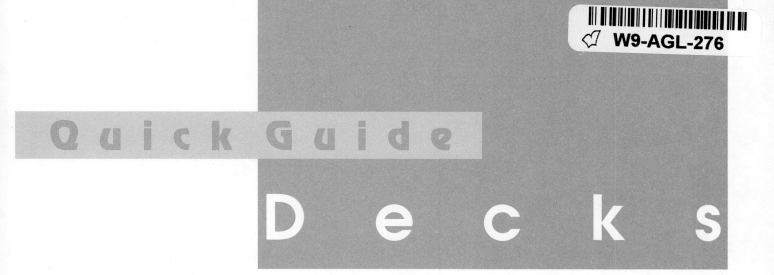

Quick Guide

Decks

CREATIVE HOMEOWNER PRESS®

COPYRIGHT © 1992
CREATIVE HOMEOWNER PRESS®
A Division of Federal Marketing Corp.
Upper Saddle River, NJ

Quick Guide is a registered trademark of Creative Homeowner Press®

Manufactured in the United States of America

Editor: Warren Ramezzana
Project Editor: Kimberly Kerrigone
Senior Designer: Annie Jeon
Illustrators: James Randolph, Norman Nuding
Production Assistant: Mindy Circelli
Technical Reviewer: Jim Barrett

Cover Design: Warren Ramezzana
Cover Illustrations: Moffit Cecil

Electronic Prepress: M. E. Aslett Corporation
Printed at: Banta Company

Current Printing (last digit)
10 9 8 7 6 5 4 3

Quick Guide: Decks
LC: 92-81619
ISBN: 1-880029-05-7 (paper)

CREATIVE HOMEOWNER PRESS®
A Division of Federal Marketing Corp.
24 Park Way
Upper Saddle River, NJ 07458

C O N T E N T S

Though all the designs and methods in this book have been tested for safety, it is not possible to overstate the importance of using the safest construction methods possible. What follows are reminders; some do's and don'ts of basic carpentry. They are not substitutes for your own common sense.

- *Always* use caution, care, and good judgment when following the procedures described in this book.

- *Always* be sure that the electrical setup is safe; be sure that no circuit is overloaded, and that all power tools and electrical outlets are properly grounded. Do not use power tools in wet locations.

- *Always* read container labels on paints, solvents, and other products; provide ventilation, and observe all other warnings.

- *Always* read the tool manufacturer's instructions for using a tool, especially the warnings.

- *Always* use holders or pushers to work pieces shorter than 3 inches on a table saw or jointer. Avoid working short pieces if you can.

- *Always* remove the key from any drill chuck (portable or press) before starting the drill.

- *Always* pay deliberate attention to how a tool works so that you can avoid being injured.

- *Always* know the limitations of your tools. Do not try to force them to do what they were not designed to do.

- *Always* make sure that any adjustment is locked before proceeding. For example, always check the rip fence on a table saw or the bevel adjustment on a portable saw before starting to work.

- *Always* clamp small pieces firmly to a bench or other work surfaces when sawing or drilling.

- *Always* wear the appropriate rubber or work gloves when handling chemicals, heavy construction or when sanding.

- *Always* wear a disposable mask when working with odors, dusts or mists. Use a special respirator when working with toxic substances.

- *Always* wear eye protection, especially when using power tools or striking metal on metal or concrete; a chip can fly off, for example, when chiseling concrete.

- *Always* be aware that there is never time for your body's reflexes to save you from injury from a power tool in a dangerous situation; everything happens too fast. Be *alert!*

- *Always* keep your hands away from the business ends of blades, cutters and bits.

- *Always* hold a portable circular saw with both hands so that you will know where your hands are.

- *Always* use a drill with an auxiliary handle to control the torque when large size bits are used.

- *Always* check your local building codes when planning new construction. The codes are intended to protect public safety and should be observed to the letter.

- *Never* work with power tools when you are tired or under the influence of alcohol or drugs.

- *Never* cut very small pieces of wood or pipe. Whenever possible, cut small pieces off larger pieces.

- *Never* change a blade or a bit unless the power cord is unplugged. Do not depend on the switch being off; you might accidentally hit it.

- *Never* work in insufficient lighting.

- *Never* work while wearing loose clothing, hanging hair, open cuffs, or jewelry.

- *Never* work with dull tools. Have them sharpened, or learn how to sharpen them yourself.

- *Never* use a power tool on a workpiece that is not firmly supported or clamped.

- *Never* saw a workpiece that spans a large distance between horses without close support on either side of the kerf; the piece can bend, closing the kerf and jamming the blade, causing saw kickback.

- *Never* support a workpiece with your leg or other part of your body when sawing.

- *Never* carry sharp or pointed tools, such as utility knives, awls, or chisels in your pocket. If you want to carry tools, use a special-purpose tool belt with leather pockets and holders.

DESIGN CHECKLIST

A deck creates an inviting extension of your indoor living space—"an outdoor room." Before you start constructing a deck, undertake a thorough investigation of the elements that will influence the design. There are some important questions you need to consider.

What do you want your deck to do for you?

How do you intend to use your deck?

How is the deck going to function with the existing site?

Functional Considerations

By answering the question "What do I want my deck to do for me?" you identify the ideas that will lead to a successful design solution. Ask yourself whether you want a very formal outdoor area primarily for entertaining large groups of people, an outdoor area only for family use, or simply a space for informally entertaining small groups of people. Will you use the deck for sunbathing or as the location of a swimming pool? Will handicapped or elderly people be using the deck? Must the deck be completely secure from the outside? Is privacy important? When you have answered these questions and considered those given below, and after you have carefully evaluated your lifestyle, you can more intelligently choose the wood deck design that will best suit your needs.

Answers for Practical Questions

How Are My Present Living Spaces Used? In answering this question, keep in mind that a deck is often best located near a kitchen area or family room. Another popular deck location is near or adjacent to the dining room. The deck should be situated near the heaviest traffic flow in the house, and it should be built in an area that can be easily modified without drastically changing the normal operation of the household. Keep in mind that the closer the deck is to your kitchen, the fewer steps you will have to take carrying food and beverages back and forth. If you prefer a small, private deck, consider building one off a bedroom or bathroom.

How Large a Deck Do I Need? There is no standard answer to this question, since individual needs vary greatly. But you should provide about 20 square feet for each person using the deck—a comfortable but not excessive space. This converts

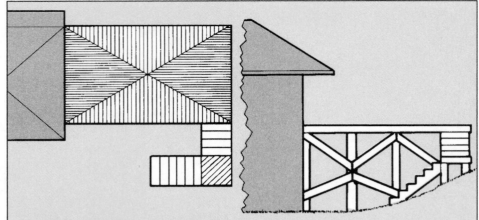

A Raised Deck On a Sloping Site. Building a deck at a higher level above a sloping site requires particular concern for proper post foundations, as well as bracing for the extended posts.

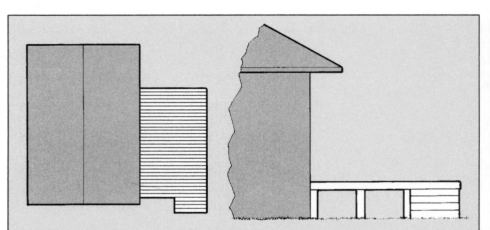

An Attached Low-Level Deck. The simplest deck to design and construct is built close to the ground, and is directly accessible from the ground floor of the house and from the surrounding yard. Plan view left, elevation right.

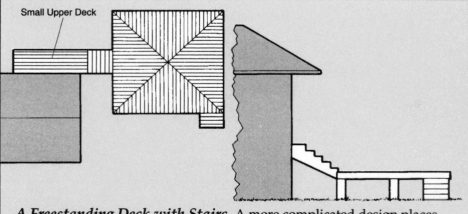

Small Upper Deck

A Freestanding Deck with Stairs. A more complicated design places the deck free of support from the house to create a more independent space. Stairs lead up to a small deck (hidden in elevation view) attached to a second story.

A Tree Top Deck for Visual Privacy. To obtain complete privacy, as well as security, build your deck up in the tree tops, attached to the second story. This creates an independent space inaccessible to intruders. Deck and railing are not attached directly to trees, to allow for wind.

A Row of Shrubs for Acoustical Privacy. A dense wall of shrubbery will cut down noise from the street or from neighbors quite effectively, without seeming to enclose the deck space.

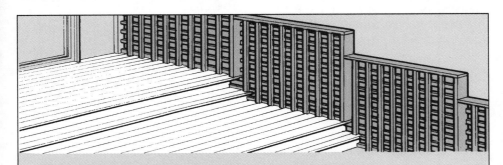

A Lattice Fence for Physical Privacy. A wooden fence of open design denies access to the deck, creates visual privacy, yet allows prevailing breezes to provide ventilation.

A Masonry Wall for Security. For the utmost in physical privacy and security, surround your deck with a masonry wall; it will also provide acoustical privacy.

to an area 4 feet by 5 feet, which provides room for a chair and space to circulate. If you regularly entertain groups of 15 to 25 people, for example, you will need 500 square feet, which is an area about 20 feet by 25 feet or the equivalent. Remember that there are limits to what a reasonably sized deck can hold. If you contemplate having groups larger than 15 to 25 people, the deck should be situated to take advantage of your site, so that the overflow can be handled without overcrowding. If the immediate area around your deck can be used by larger groups, you might find that a smaller deck will function far more efficiently than a grandiose one. Be realistic about your space needs. Often a clever arrangement of furniture or plants can give the impression of a much larger space and yet preserve the charm of a more intimate area.

Your choice of a ground-level or an elevated deck will be determined partly by the configuration of your site and by access to the deck from your house and the site. A deck situated on a second-floor level is often the only alternative available on a steeply sloping site. A deck at ground level, however, can provide a larger surface, which might be required to accommodate your particular needs and your site. It also offers a wider choice of construction materials.

How Will I Use the Deck? Decide first whether you need a formal or informal area. A deck subjected to continual wear and tear from children and pets must be sturdy as well as suitable for adult needs. An informal arrangement, constructed of relatively heavy-duty materials and incorporating built-in furniture, is often the best choice for such a deck. It requires less attention to details and gives more layout options. A formal deck is usually less subject to hard, constant use, and so it would be appropriate to consider lighter weight materials, movable outdoor furniture, and decorative details such as trellises and flowerbox borders.

Do I Want Privacy? The openness of a deck depends on how much privacy you want. While there are other considerations that affect the degree of openness, the need for privacy often dictates the final design solution. Keep in mind that there are three types of privacy: visual, acoustical, and physical. Defining each of these three types is important because you may be concerned with one, two, or all three. Each requires a specific architectural treatment. Special considerations for each type of privacy are explained below.

Visual Privacy. Ask yourself: Is protection from being seen, or from seeing others, necessary? You may discover that the most desirable exposure for your deck faces an unsightly yard, street, or railroad tracks—not to mention the houses or apartments nearby that look into your outdoor space. Here are some recommendations to correct these conditions.

A simple wood fence high enough to screen out the undesirable view, or a low-brick or decorative concrete block wall used in conjunction with vertical shrubs can create an effective screen. Rows of shrubs of varying height can limit the view into and out of your space. A lattice covered with ivy or similar creeping vines is another effective screening technique.

Acoustical Privacy. Do you need protection from unwanted or bothersome noises? While no method is perfect, acoustical isolation—using readily available materials and landscaping—in most instances can offer sufficient protection from distracting noises. One method that is attractive and effective makes use of plantings of shrubs or evergreens. For example, evergreens placed across the path of the noise source will break up the noise so that it will merge with background noises. A fence or wall, in combination with

vertical evergreens or shrubs, gives additional isolation from noise sources that are exceptionally severe. Since it is impossible to stop all noise from penetrating your outdoor area, keep in mind that an exterior deck is by its nature open. The more you enclose your deck, the more likely it is that it will lose its original desirability.

Physical Privacy. This includes protection from intrusion by unwanted guests or pets, and can also be thought of as security. While fences with controlled access or lockable gates prevent strangers from wandering in off the streets, low walls with evergreen shrubs may provide all the physical privacy you need.

To accurately evaluate your needs, you must answer the following questions: Do you want to control access to your deck? What kind of security do you want or need? This will depend in part on whether or not the deck is enclosed in any manner. Do you need a method of keeping youngsters out of or inside the area? Are there mandatory requirements for fences in your area?

Site Considerations

When you have clearly identified what functions you want your deck to fulfill, the next step is to understand the physical and environmental limitations of your site. These restrictions have as much influence over the physical design of your deck as your functional requirements. It is essential that you evaluate the following considerations.

Terrain. The location of your deck and the type of structure you choose may be dictated by the terrain. A flat area with firm, stable soil will require a minimum of support. If the terrain pitches either toward or away from the house, then posts, footings, and bracing will have to be more elaborate. The slope of the terrain in

relation to your house is very important in determining the design and structure of your deck.

Utilities. Before starting any deck construction, it is essential to determine the location of all utility lines, both underground and aboveground. Water, gas, sewer and telephone lines running under your intended deck area will influence your planning. Special construction may be necessary, or either the lines or the deck may have to be relocated. Accidents can easily occur as a result of not knowing where and at what depth the lines are located.

To locate these lines, check with the customer service departments of your local utility companies. They will help you determine the precise location of their service installations on your property. They may also suggest ways of building over or around the problem. If your house was built recently, your local building inspector will probably have a copy of your utility, gas, water and sewer hookup locations. Keep this information in your files for future reference. It may be that no connections or underground lines exist under or near the proposed deck site. Most often, utility lines are located in a zone from $2\frac{1}{2}$ to 8 feet below ground level. Normally, the major concern is that the location of deep footings will conflict with the utility service.

You can see the path of any aboveground, overhead utility lines, such as telephone or electric wires. You probably will not want to locate a deck directly beneath them, especially if you plan to construct a roof structure.

Soil Conditions. Even if soil conditions around your house are normally stable, remember that minor excavation should be filled in as soon as possible to reduce settlement of surrounding soil into the excavation. Soils with a high clay content tend to swell during the spring; this can cause movement of the deck. Get professional help to solve difficult soil problems. Most other types of soil are considered quite stable for deck support.

Plants and Trees. In planning an outdoor space, take inventory of the existing plants and trees in the construction area. Evaluate the relative condition and the survival ability of each plant or tree before you decide to move it to another location. (Your local nursery or grower can advise you about the hardiness of any particular plant or tree.) Remember that a minimum of transplanting and cutting is the most satisfactory course; this reduces your total replacement costs. To move a mature tree that is located where you want a deck is impractical, and cutting the tree down is not a good solution. Instead, design the deck to include the tree by leaving an opening around the trunk. Once you have chosen a deck location, make a sketch of the area and mark those plants or trees that can be kept and those that must be moved.

Pools. If you are planning a pool as part of your deck design, locate the closest water supply source. It is important to minimize the length of run of pipe required to service the pool. In northern climates, make sure that the water pipe can be pitched from a high to a low level so it can be drained. Your pool contractor can advise you on safety restrictions on pool access.

Electrical Needs. Lines to supply deck electrical outlets and lighting must be planned well in advance of construction. The need for an underground cable from your main service panel or the possibility of through-the-wall connection should be considered when planning the location of the deck.

Zoning & Code Requirements

Zoning. Zoning laws control land use and the density of building in prescribed areas. They specify setback requirements, which state how close you can build to any property line, the height of fences and trellises, and in some cases, what materials may be used. They may specify how much of your lot may be covered by structures.

If your plans conflict with regulations, you can apply for a variance, that is, a permit to build a structure that does not conform in detail to the law. Do not put up a structure that violates your local zoning laws and codes. A building inspector's report could lead to a legal order to tear it down.

Determine whether there are any easements spelled out in the property deed. An easement is a right-of-way granted to a utility company or other property owner. Your deed may include other stipulations that limit the design or the location of a new structure. Check your deed before you build.

Codes. Building codes are intended to protect public safety. Although local requirements may vary, most building codes stipulate that all exterior decks not in direct contact with the ground must be able to support at least 60 pounds per square foot. This figure takes into account the effect of snow loads in northern climates as well as the effect of a large group of people standing on the deck. All design recommendations and sizes found in this book have been calculated to meet that loading requirement. Building codes also stipulate that second-story railings on the exterior of the house must be either 36 inches or 42 inches. Before construction begins, you must obtain a building permit from your local building inspector's office. This office may require one or more sets of your plans. When reviewing your plan, the inspector will make sure that your proposed design and construction meet all applicable codes.

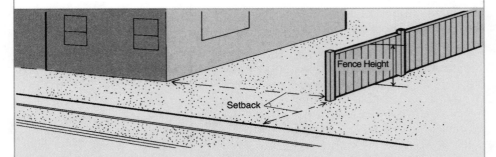

Local codes may restrict the locations and dimensions of fences and other structures in relation to the street or to next door neighbors.

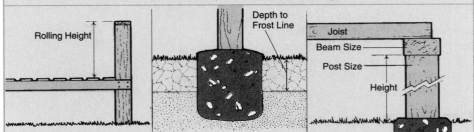

Local building codes may specify what railing heights you must use, how far below the frost line post foundations must go, as well as the sizes of the wood structural members of your deck.

Climatic Considerations

Environmental and physical factors that affect the amount and type of light, the volume and direction of wind, and the control of rain and snowfall all have a profound influence on your deck design.

Orientation. First, decide in what direction your outdoor space will face. This will affect the amount of sun and shade the deck will receive (see figures right).

A north-facing space in the Northern Hemisphere will be in shade most of the day. While this is the most desirable exposure in a southern climate, it could be cold and uncomfortable in a northern climate. In colder or more severe climates, a southwest exposure provides full afternoon and late afternoon sun. This will make your outdoor space usable as long as possible and keep it warmer on many cool spring and fall days.

The activities you are planning for the deck can influence its orientation. Evaluate your needs regarding the quality and quantity of light. North sky light is far more diffused than direct sunlight.

The position of the sun in the sky and the angle of the sun should also be considered. The angle of the sun is higher during the summer months than the winter months. If you are considering a fence or other obstacle on the southern side of your deck, keep in mind that it may block a considerable amount of the low-angle sunlight during the winter. However, sunlight will fall across most of the outdoor area during the summer. Especially in southern regions, overhead trellises or lanais are used to control the amount of direct sun.

Wind. If your site has a breeze during the entire day, some form of windbreak is called for (see figures page 11). Planning to accommodate the wind's movements means observing the wind pattern around

Summer Sun & Shade

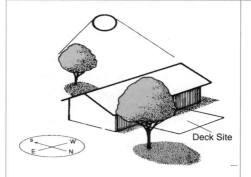

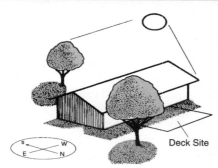

In the Northern Hemisphere, the noonday summer sun stands high in the sky: buildings and trees cast little shadow.

The late afternoon summer sun is as far to the north as it will go: there will be minimal shade on the north and east of buildings.

Spring & Autumn Sun & Shade

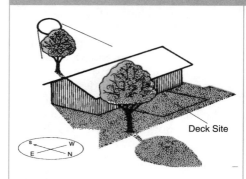

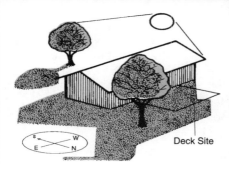

The noonday sun in spring and autumn is partway to its zenith: buildings cast considerable shadows, as do fully-leafed trees.

The late afternoon spring and autumn sun is fairly low in the sky: there is much shadow on the north and east sides of buildings.

Winter Sun & Shade

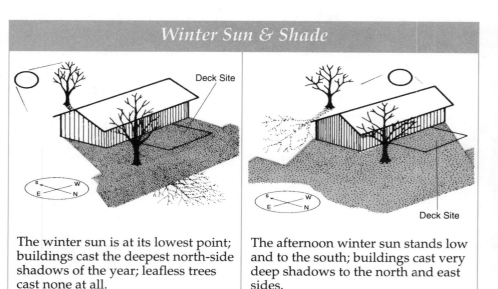

The winter sun is at its lowest point; buildings cast the deepest north-side shadows of the year; leafless trees cast none at all.

The afternoon winter sun stands low and to the south; buildings cast very deep shadows to the north and east sides.

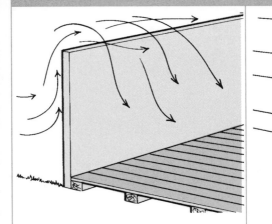

A solid wall deflects most breezes over the deck, while allowing gentle ventilation near the wall.

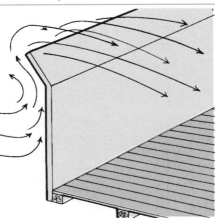

A louvered wall lets all air currents through to the deck; slanting the louvers up or down can direct the breezes as you desire.

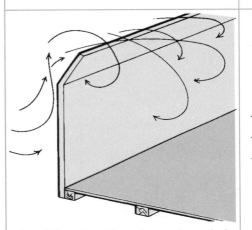

A solid wall with an inward-angled extension draws air currents down, creating movement near the wall.

A solid wall with an outward-angled extension deflects air currents up and over the deck, creating a still area near the wall.

Panels in a acrylic-walled deck can be hinged to permit any desired degree of ventilation by prevailing winds.

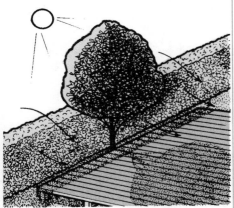

Shrubbery and trees will deflect and moderate prevailing winds, allowing some gentle ventilation of deck areas.

your house. Recall where the leaves collect in the fall; this might indicate a zone of little air movement.

In southern climates, air movement is a definite advantage. Air moving under a shade device feels cooler than a breeze in direct sunlight. The cooling effect will be more noticeable from a sunshade located on the windward side of the house. Breezes are easily directed and controlled by appropriate placement of screens, fences, or hedges. In zones where air movement is minimal, locate the deck so that air will be funneled through the deck structure.

Rain and Snow. Rainfall and snow on a deck can have damaging consequences. If the deck is not pitched to shed water, ponding or puddling can result. Rainfall and snow are particularly detrimental to your house if the roof is pitched toward the deck. In some cases minor flooding can occur, especially if the deck is on the same level as the house. This is why it is wise to make the deck level a few inches lower than the adjoining interior floor level. If the decking will run perpendicular (with the ends at the house side), will be laid without spacing, or will be covered with exterior-grade carpeting, then the deck must slope away from the house 1/4 inch per foot. Be sure adjacent areas can handle rain runoff from the deck.

Weathering. All materials tend to decay under the influence of weathering. Thus the appearance of the materials you use to construct your deck will change naturally over the years. Each material has its own patina of weathering. A well-selected group of materials may look incompatible during construction, but will blend together in a most pleasing manner after they have weathered.

Freezing and Thawing. The freezing and thawing that occur in northern climates can severely damage building materials. The use of expansion joints, caulking, and proper weather protection of susceptible materials will reduce decay due to winter or wet-weather conditions.

Choosing a Deck Material

A deck intended for do-it-yourself construction should use materials that are lightweight and capable of spanning small distances without excessive bending. A deck is either directly beside—and usually attached to—a house, or is freestanding, away from a house. Except for cantilevered construction, a deck needs a foundation to support it in the ground, which requires two types of materials—one for the superstructure and another for the foundation. Keep the architecture, materials, and the decoration of your house in mind when choosing deck materials. If the materials of both house and deck are compatible, this will produce a natural transition between the interior of the house and the exterior deck. The major criteria for selecting deck materials are these: They should be in keeping with the surrounding architecture. They should be available locally in pleasing colors and textures. They should require low maintenance and be economically feasible.

Wood. Wood is the most popular and basic deck material. The visual qualities of wood—its grain, texture, and color— make it an exciting material to work with. Since all deck wood is used in an exterior application, it must have good weathering qualities and be free of rot and insect infestation. Cypress, spruce, and redwood possess excellent weathering durability, and if left unpainted will gradually acquire a soft, attractive, gray patina. Wood preservatives and pressure-treated wood, for exterior use, are available at lumberyards; their use will improve the durability of any deck. The design possibilities offered by wood are endless; floorboard patterns, spacings, edgings, and railings all offer scope for your creative imagination. Wood construction patterns may appear complex, but they are fairly simple for a homeowner to build. Wood structural components are available in a variety of sizes, shapes, and textures. Local lumberyards display a wide range of materials to help you make a selection. Be sure to select wood that will weather to a desired color and patina. Newly installed wood looks very different from its later, weathered condition. Make sure you see samples of wood that has weathered in an exposure like the one your deck will experience. If you do not, you might be very disappointed in a few years. Wood can also be painted or stained to integrate the deck with the color scheme of the house (wait six months before painting treated wood). Since the paint will cover most of the blemishes, a lower grade of material can be used. Wood can be fastened with a variety of connectors: nails, bolts, screws, and metal plates.

Types of Decking. Almost any design for decking is possible. However, the more elaborate the design, the more work involved, especially in providing adequate joist support for all decking pieces. Wood decking comes in several sizes and species. Do not use decking wider than 6 in. Using narrower widths minimizes cupping and the potential for splitting along the board. Normally, 2x6 wood decking will span a joist spacing of 4 ft. 2x4 decking will span 3 ft. if laid on its side and run for more than two joist spaces. Most 1x4 and 1x6 decking will span no more than 16 in. without flexing when laid flat and continued over more than two spans. In any case, the shorter the span, the stiffer the deck. If you plan to have unusual loads on the deck, such as heavy furniture, these recommendations are not applicable; in this case, you should call in an architect or contractor.

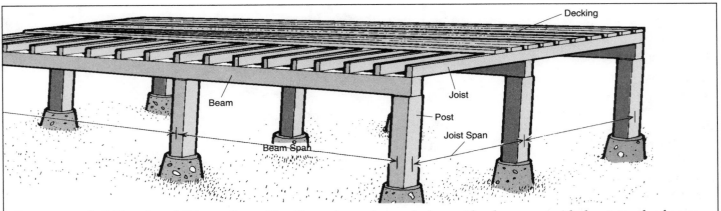

Recommended Structural Dimensions. The dimensions of your deck must be drawn up with the strength of your lumber in mind. Check with the lumberyard first as to availability and cost; then use the charts below for planning.

Recommended Beam Spans (length of beam between posts)

Species	Beam Size	4'	5'	6'	7'	8'	9'	10'	11'
Group I	4 x 6	Up to 6'							
	3 x 8	Up to 8'		7'	6'				
	4 x 8	Up to 10'	9'	8'	7'		6'		
	3 x 10	Up to 11'	10'	9'	8'		7'		6'
	4 x 10	Up to 12'	11'	10'	9'		8'		7'
	3 x 12	Up to	12'	11'	10'	9'		8'	
	4 x 12	Up to	12'		11'	10'		9'	
Group II	4 x 6	Up to 6'							
	3 x 8	Up to 7'		6'					
	4 x 8	Up to 9'	8'	7'		6'			
	3 x 10	Up to 10'	9'	8'	7'		6'		
	4 x 10	Up to 11'	10'	9'	8'		7'		
	3 x 12	Up to 12'	11'	10'	9'	8'		7'	
	4 x 12	Up to	12'		11'	10'	9'		8'

Recommended Maximum Joist Spans

Species	Joist Size	16" Spacing	24" Spacing	32" Spacing
Group I	2 x 6	9' 9"	8' 6"	7' 9"
Group II	2 x 6	8' 7"	7' 6"	6' 10"
Group I	2 x 8	12' 10"	11' 3"	10' 2"
Group II	2 x 8	11' 4"	9' 11"	9' 0"
Group I	2 x 10	16' 5"	14' 4"	13' 0"
Group II	2 x 10	14' 6"	12' 8"	11' 6"

Example: A 2 x 8 joist from Group II, using 24" joist spacing, should span no more than 9'11".

Strength Ratings of Wood Species

Ratings refer to lumber grade No. 1 or better.

Group I (strongest)
Douglas Fir
Western Hemlock
Western Larch
Southern Pine
Coast Sitka Spruce

Group II
Western Cedar
Douglas Fir (southern)
White Fir
Eastern Hemlock

Creating the Design

The following design specifics will help you create the perfect deck.

Shape. Select a familiar geometric shape such as a square, rectangle, triangle, hexagon, or circle for your deck. The physical features of the site should determine which of these shapes would best fit.

Material Compatibility. Your basic materials, textures, and colors should be in keeping with those of your house or the architecture of the surrounding area. Try to limit your selection to no more than two materials.

Deck Level. There are several types of construction to choose from, depending on the terrain of your site.

Deck on Grade. This is suitable for a level site with a minimum of obstacles; a wood deck built just above grade is recommended. It is often built at or just below the interior floor level (right).

A deck on grade can be attached to the main house or it can be freestanding. Deciding which is the best often depends on the type of house construction and its material—wood is easy to join to; brick is much more difficult. A freestanding deck can be placed almost anywhere within a site.

Raised Deck. Access to the site is usually provided by exterior stairs. Building codes often require that a raised deck have two means of entrance or exit. A deck on a sloping site can step down in a series of platforms. A stepped deck is basically a combination of several smaller decks connected together.

Multi-Level Deck on Sloping Sites. Where the terrain rises away from the house, you can terrace the slope to the desired level. Thus the outer part of the deck will be on grade, and the rest can be elevated to this level. The deck should be accessible directly at the house level.

The simplest deck design rests directly on the ground, without any elaborate or expensive support structure.

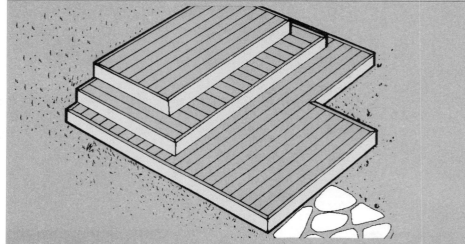

A visually more intersting form of simple deck combines ground-level sections with raised sections.

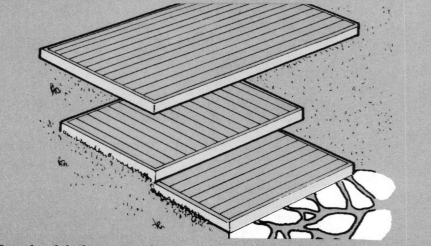

Low-level decks are simple to construct; multilevel design creates visual interest, while adapting to site requirements.

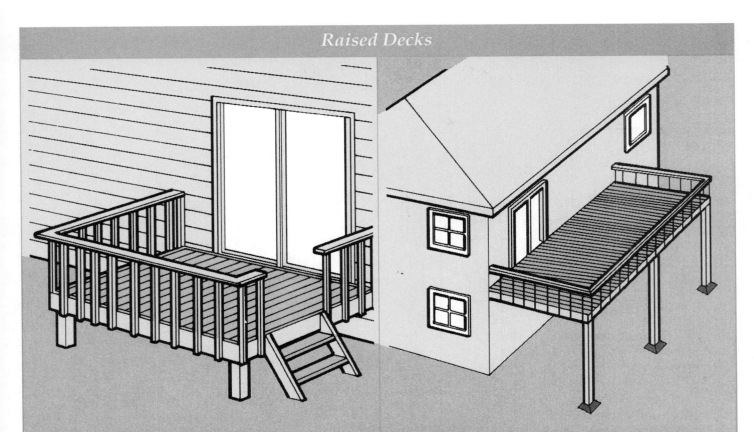

The most common deck design stands 2 to 4 ft. off the ground, is attached on one side to a house, and includes stairs to reach the ground.

A raised deck can be built at practically any height if adequate support is provided by existing structures and strong posts with proper footings.

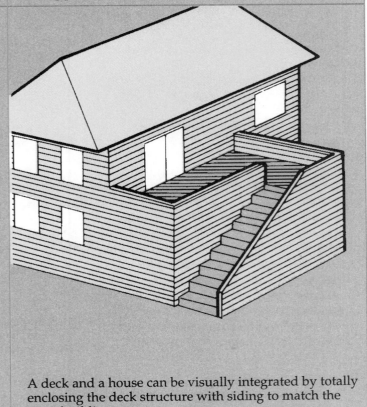

An elevated deck may be built on top of an existing building, using it for the necessary support structure.

A deck and a house can be visually integrated by totally enclosing the deck structure with siding to match the main building.

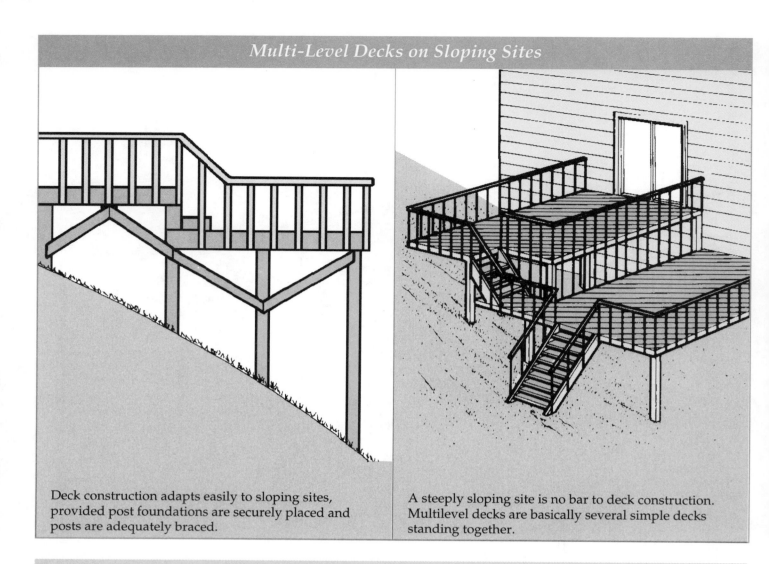

Deck construction adapts easily to sloping sites, provided post foundations are securely placed and posts are adequately braced.

A steeply sloping site is no bar to deck construction. Multilevel decks are basically several simple decks standing together.

Deck with Cantilever Construction

There are some sites that slope so steeply that you cannot support an extended deck on the site itself. The most obvious solution to this problem is to construct a cantilevered deck, one in which all supports are attached or connected to the house—nothing extends to the ground. This requires a much more complex design and building procedure than for a normal site construction, since the house must be capable of supporting the added weight of the deck and the people and furniture placed on it. Consult an architect, engineer, or contractor to work out the technical details required by this kind of construction. It is likely that much of the work will have to be done by professionals.

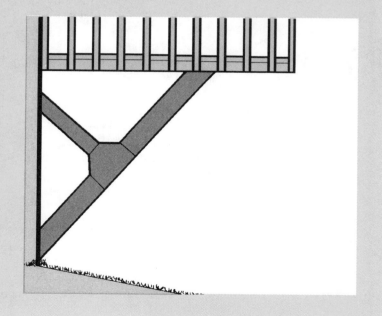

DEVELOPING A SITE PLAN

Design ideas must be drawn out clearly so that you can obtain the necessary building permits and estimate the quantities of materials needed to build the deck.

The first step is to create a measured drawing of the site, including the existing structures, lot lines, easements, underground utilities, water lines, and, of course, the proposed deck. The procedure is simple but requires an accurate recording of what exists on the site.

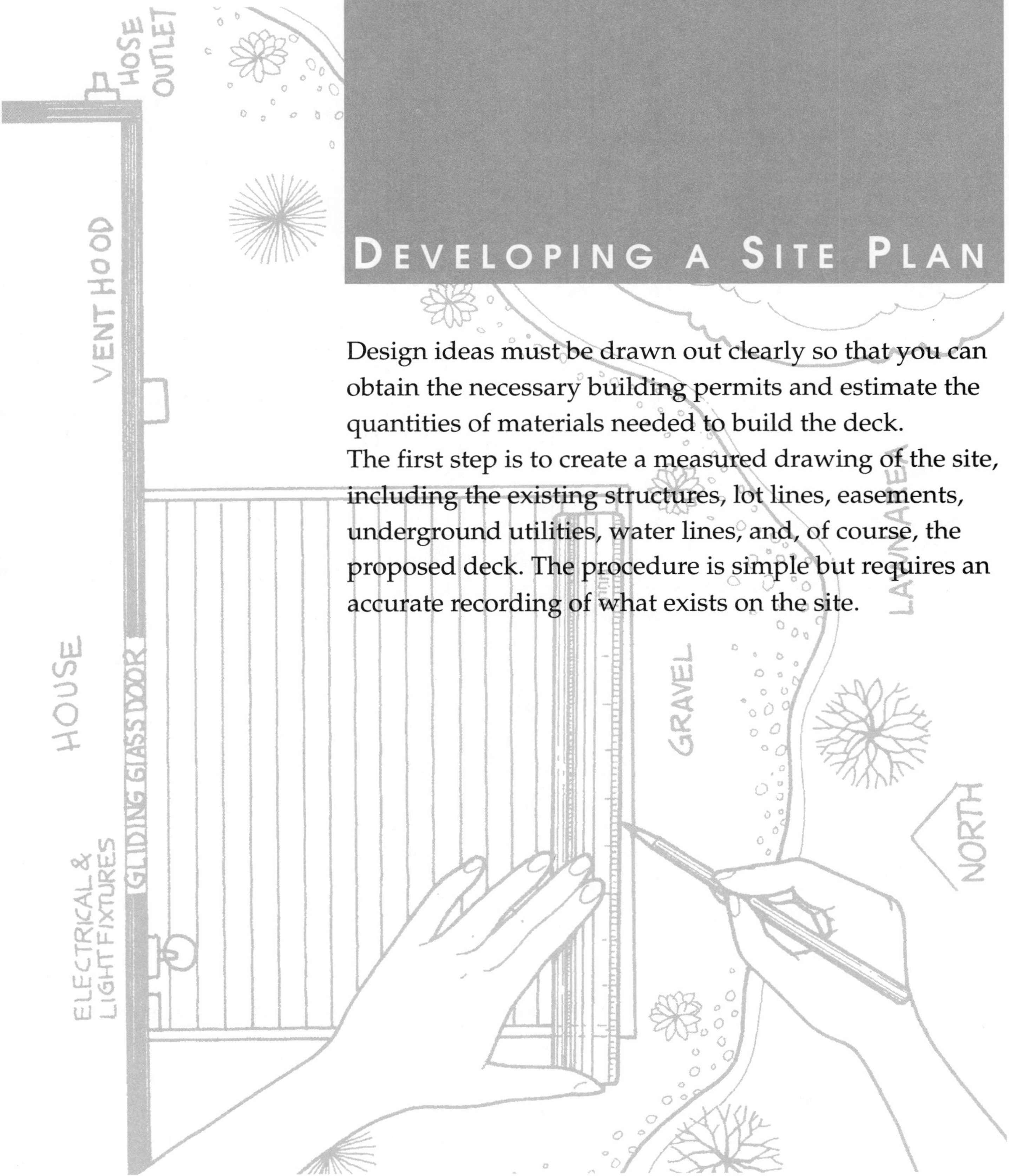

HOSE OUTLET

VENT HOOD

HOUSE

GLIDING GLASS DOOR

ELECTRICAL & LIGHT FIXTURES

LAWN AREA

GRAVEL

NORTH

Drawing the Plan

Follow these steps in drawing your plan on grid paper.

1 Establishing a Scale. Select an outside corner of your house at the foundation line as the reference point for all subsequent measurements. From this corner, measure the dimensions and locations of all existing and proposed structures and plantings to be plotted on the grid.

Establish a drawing scale by setting a value on 1/4, 1/2, 1, or 2 feet for each grid square. If you use a scale of 1/4 inch equal to 1 foot, then a measurement of 10 feet along your foundation wall would be marked 10 grid squares long on your plan. Choose a scale that will put your entire plan on no more than one or two sheets of grid paper.

2 Marking the Exposures. Measure the entire foundation of your house and draw it on the grid. Mark north, south, east and west exposures.

Mark, in an upper page corner, the north arrow, plus east, west, and south. Mark the directions from which the prevailing summer and winter winds blow.

3 Measuring the Room Dimensions. Locate the interior room that will connect with the deck. Measure from the original reference corner around the outside of the house until you come to a window, door, or joint that is also part of that room. Measure the room dimensions from that point and mark them on the scale drawing.

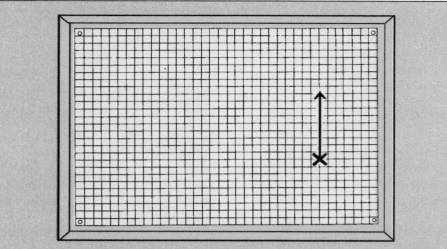

1 Use a large sheet of grid paper. Decide what scale you will use; a 1/4 in. on the paper equaling 1 foot on the ground is standard. The "X" marks the house corner where measuring starts.

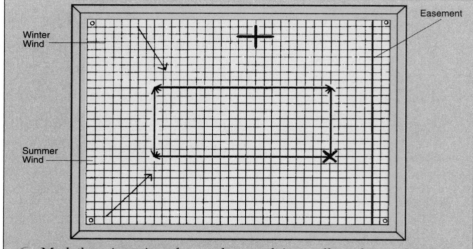

2 Mark the orientation of your plan; north is usually at the top. Measure the dimensions of your house and other structures and mark them on the paper, beginning at the "X".

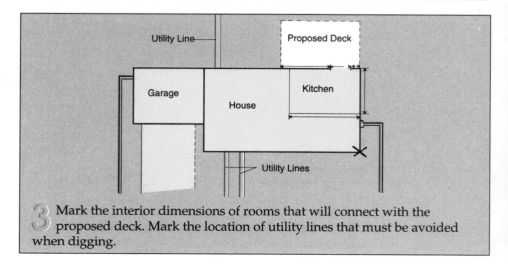

3 Mark the interior dimensions of rooms that will connect with the proposed deck. Mark the location of utility lines that must be avoided when digging.

4 Locating Utilities. From the information gathered from local utilities, mark down the positions of all pipes and wires. This will reveal any conflict between your deck design ideas and any underground or overhead utilities.

Next, mark the boundaries and corners of your property. You may have to add some paper to include your entire lot drawn to scale. Mark the lot lines, the setback lines that local zoning requires, and any easements that are part of your deed.

5 Marking the Landscaping. Mark the positions of all trees and shrubs that will be kept and those that will have to be removed or relocated. This will indicate the shady areas and help in estimating the amount of landscaping work required. Make several photocopies of this plan so you can try more than one deck design and layout.

6 Drawing the Deck. Now draw in the plan of the proposed deck, including stairs, railings and any other elements. It is helpful to compare several plan arrangements, drawn on various copies of the site plan, so that you can visualize the size and shape, and begin to estimate quantities and materials needed. Now is the time to discover potential problems with your plan. Be sure the spacing of posts, beams, and joists follows the recommendations given on page 13.

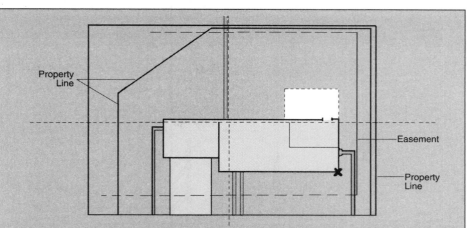

4 Mark property lines, easements, buried utility lines, septic systems and any building code restriction. Setbacks from property lines should be specific.

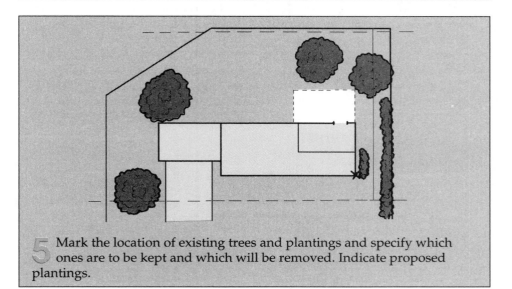

5 Mark the location of existing trees and plantings and specify which ones are to be kept and which will be removed. Indicate proposed plantings.

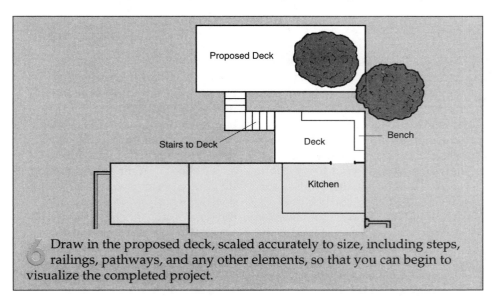

6 Draw in the proposed deck, scaled accurately to size, including steps, railings, pathways, and any other elements, so that you can begin to visualize the completed project.

Drawing the Details

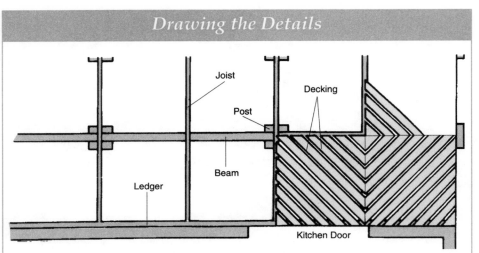

Once you are settled on your design, draw up the plan at a larger scale, perhaps 1 inch equal to 1 foot. To do this, simply convert all previous measurements to the new scale. For example, if you measured 10 feet on the ground, that would convert to 40 grid squares on your plan at the larger scale. This drawing can be limited to the deck and the immediate area, including portions of the house and other structures or significant features, such as a pool or paths. Also include trees, flower beds and shrubs. This larger scale plan will help you visualize the patterns of your design as well as the relative size of the project.

Drawing the Elevation

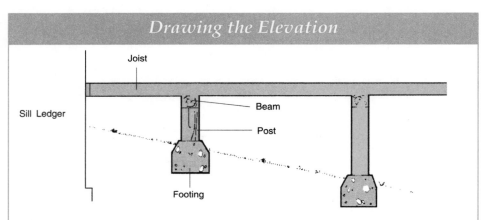

After you have made a plan of your deck at a scale large enough for all the details to be indicated, you are ready to draw an elevation— a vertical picture at the same large scale. If your deck is attached to the house, measure vertically from a horizontal line on your foundation or from a floor line that shows on the outside, to find the height of all openings, vents, eaves, roof lines and such. Mark these, as well as the ground level, on your scale elevation. If your deck is not connected to the house, indicate only the ground level. Add an elevation drawing (side view) of your proposed deck, including railings, stairs, and connections to other structures that you plan to build. All this information is necessary for estimating material needs. Most building inspectors and the local building departments that grant permits will accept a well-drawn plan and elevation of the type described above with your application for a permit. If they require a more architectural plan, a local drafting service or an architectural firm can provide the necessary help.

Estimating Materials

Use the completed plans of your proposed deck to make a list of all materials needed. Include the quantities and dimensions of each size of lumber; for example, 12 4x4 8-foot posts, 36 2x6 10-foot joists. Since there is some waste when installing decking and railings, add about 5 percent to your estimate of materials for these components. For example, if you figure you need 38 2x4s, buy two or three extra to be on the safe side.

Include post footings, cement mix, fasteners (nails, bolts, and screws), connectors (joist hangers, post anchors), and any wood preservatives and stains that you will need.

When calculating lumber quantities, remember that, although you draw up plans in actual dimensions, you buy lumber in nominal sizes. For example, a 2x10 actually measures $1\frac{1}{2} \times 9\frac{1}{2}$ inches.

Use the following method to estimate the quantity of decking you will need: Find the number of 2x4s needed to fill a given deck width by multiplying the deck width in feet by 3.4. (The deck width is the dimension of the deck that is at right angles to the direction in which the 2x4s are laid.) For example, to fill 12 feet of deck width with 2x4s, figure 12x3.4=40 (rounded off) plus 5 percent for waste = about 43. If your deck is 16 feet long, you need 43 16-foot 2x4s. However, 2x4s are sold in 6, 8, and 12-foot lengths. In this case, you would buy about 86 8-foot 2x4s. If you plan to use 2x6s for your deck flooring, use a factor of 2.1 instead of 3.4 to find the number of pieces needed.

When you are ready to buy lumber, keep in mind that most suppliers price lumber by the linear foot; that is, a one-foot-long piece of whatever type or size you need.

DECK BUILDING BASICS

Before starting the construction of a deck, identify clearly all those pieces that will make up the finished deck. Every deck consists of two major sections:

1. Above-grade elements such as decking, joists, beams, ledgers, railings and benches;

2. Below-grade or supporting elements such as posts, piers and footings.

Parts of a Deck

All weights and loads that are imposed on a deck are directly supported by the decking. While the decking might appear to be decorative, its main function is to transfer all the weight and load to the joists. Joists are the primary structural element supporting the deck floor. They are best described as closely spaced structural members that support the deck which in turn are supported by horizontal beams. The beams are larger elements that gather the load and weight of the joists resting on them and transfer it to the posts. The posts are vertical supports spaced at appropriate intervals to transfer all the load from the beams directly into the ground through the footings.

Footings, which bear all the weight of the deck, are set into the soil to distribute the weight uniformly. In low-profile decks built 6 to 18 inches above the ground, the beams themselves may rest on the footings, thus eliminating the need for posts.

Decking. The major visual element of a deck is the decking, the surface you stand on. It is the most interesting part of the deck because of its pattern and detailing. The decking pattern also determines the spacing of the joists, which in turn affects the beams and the footings. Therefore, the pattern you select must be coordinated with a suitable structural framing plan. Most wood decking can be applied in many patterns, the most common being parallel, diagonal, diamond, radial and parquet. The most-often-used

grade of lumber is No. 2 Common (see chart on page 13). The most popular species used for decking are redwood, cedar, hemlock, fir and pine. In order to satisfy local building codes for exterior decks, all decking should be supported by joists no farther apart than 24 inches on center. If you plan to have heavy weights on the decking, the spacing should be 16 inches on center. Almost all decking material is laid flat; that is, on its broad side. This means that the 2-inch nominal dimension of the decking is the depth, and the 4- or 6-inch dimension is the wearing surface. For a finer-lined, more narrowly patterned deck, you can set the 2x4s on edge instead of flat. Of course, more material will be used, at greater expense. Decking boards are usually

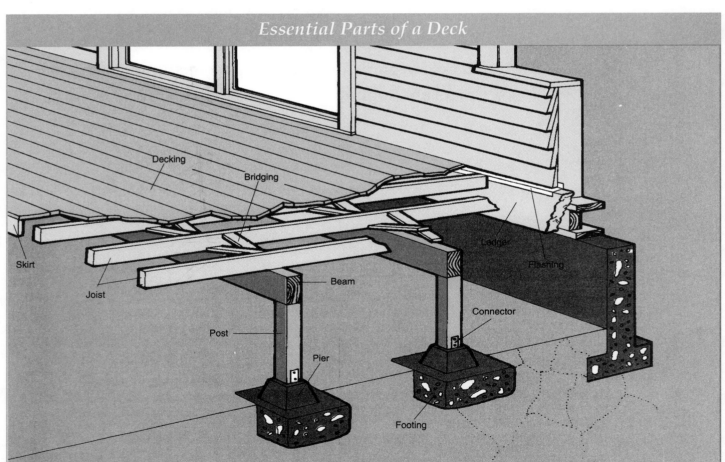

Essential Parts of a Deck

Decking

Bridging

Skirt

Joist

Post

Pier

Beam

Connector

Footing

Ledger

Flashing

Standard wood deck construction uses the parts shown here, arranged so that the decking—the visible component—is supported by larger and more widely spaced members, including joists, beams, posts, piers, and at the bottom, footings. In this example, the ledger beam secures one side of the deck to an existing structure.

spaced about 1/8 to 1/4 inch apart to let rain and dirt pass through to the ground. Because the layout of the decking determines the layout of the supporting structure, first choose the deck pattern you want, then the grade of material and the type, and finally the spacing of the joists.

Joists. The joists bear the full brunt of the load from the decking. They are supported at each end (and perhaps in the middle) by beams and they span the space between the beams. Joist spacing is usually dictated by the spanning and load-bearing capacity of the joist rather than by spacing imposed by the decking. The chart on page 13 gives joist span limits for different sizes of joists. Most joists are 2-inch wood and the most common sizes are 2x6, 2x8 and 2x10. Joists are

attached to beams or a ledger by nails or metal connectors (see page 27). Joists can be cantilevered out beyond each supporting beam for a distance of one-quarter of the span. This flexibility lets you derive maximum use of the material and gives you greater design flexibility. For example, joists spanning 10 feet from support to support can be as long as 15 feet overall (one-quarter of the 10-foot span is 2½ feet, so this much extension can be made at both ends of the joist). Such extensions can be made without increasing the size of the joists or the spacing. In any case, it is a good idea to insert crossbracing between the joists, to increase the overall stiffness of the joist and deck assembly. Some local codes require the use of crossbracing or bridging.

Beams. The beams are the heavier structural elements that support the joists. The size of the beam required depends on beam spacing and the spacing of the beam supports, that is, the posts and footings. In general, the trade-off between beam thickness and the number of supports is as follows: It is less expensive and time-consuming to have a thicker beam than it is to have more posts and footings. Often, beams are constructed by bolting or nailing together the same materials used for joists, which are smaller or thinner, to make the necessary larger size. This form of built-up beam is a standard construction technique. Beams are fastened to the posts or footings by metal connectors or cleats. These are available at most lumberyards or home supply stores.

Variations of Decking Patterns

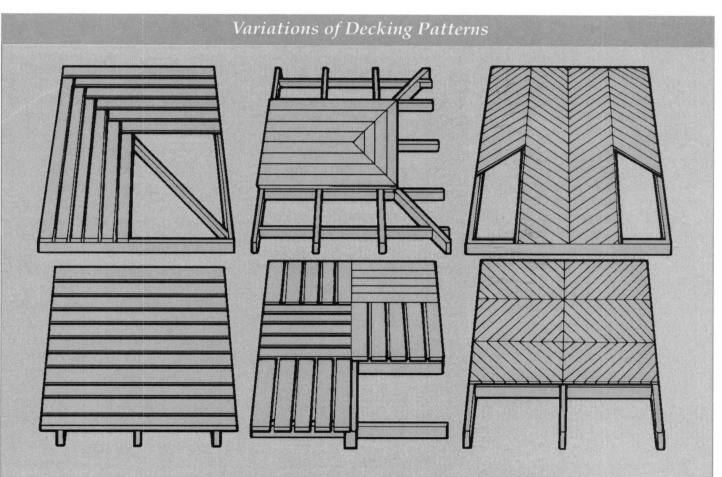

Decking materials can be laid down in almost any desired pattern, as long as sufficient support is provided by underlying joists, especially at the ends of the decking pieces.

Beams can be cantilevered out from the posts to create an overhang. The same limit applies as for the joists—no more than 1/4 span beyond an end support.

Ledgers. If the deck is attached to the side of a house or other building, then the framing construction uses the existing building as one support. A ledger strip attached to the house supports the joists that are attached to it. Usually a ledger is a 2-inch-thick piece of wood (occasionally a steel beam is used) that is attached to the house by bolts, nails, or metal connectors. Another way to attach the joists is by using a metal angle strip, normally 3x3 inches. This is attached to the house with bolts or a similar device, and the joist ends rest on and are attached to the angle. It is important to set the ledger strip so that the joists and the finished decking are at least 1 to 2 inches below the interior floor level. This will reduce the possibility of rain or snow entering the house. The minimum recommendation is to lower the decking 1 inch. If rain and snow conditions are unlikely or very infrequent in your area, the decking can be placed flush with the interior floor level.

Posts. The posts transfer the combined weight of the decking, joists, beams, and the user loads to the footings or the foundation. Most decks use 4x4 posts, but this size must be increased when posts support a structure higher than 6 feet above grade. A larger size is also required if the site slopes away from the house, or where heavy loads are expected. In addition, posts that have to support overhead cover or a roof must be larger than 4x4. Check your local building code for legal requirements and specific recommendations. Posts are connected to the footings or foundations either by being directly embedded in the concrete or by means of mechanical

connectors. If your deck stands high off the ground, diagonal bracing is usually required to increase the stability of the deck. Crossbracing can be effectively integrated into the deck design by extending the pieces up to the height of the railing or by creating diagonal latticework around the base. Local building codes often dictate the bracing requirements.

Footings. The footings are the final destination of all the loads and forces supported by the decking, joists, beams, and posts. Local building codes are very specific about requirements for foundations. Ideally, footings should be constructed on undisturbed soil or on rock. If this is not possible, the soil should be compacted by tamping, using a mechanized or hand tamper. The footings must extend below the frost line, which varies in different parts of the country from a minimum depth of 24 inches to a maximum of 48 inches.

Local conditions may require special procedures; consult your building department. Footings are usually made of poured-in-place concrete. They can be rectangular, circular, or square, depending on the connection and framework you've chosen. Footings should extend at least 2 to 6 inches out of the ground so that the post does not come in contact with the soil. This also lets rain drain rapidly away from the post and its point of contact with the footing. Where the posts are embedded in concrete rather than attached with metal connectors, the posts must be treated to prevent rot and insect damage. Old telephone poles make excellent posts for embedding in concrete. For low-level decks, concrete blocks or precast footings can be placed on compacted soil. However, this method does not guarantee that settlement will not occur.

Building Permits

The position and design of the deck with regard to the house is influenced by specific building and legal requirements, and in turn influences the choice of materials and the estimate of quantities needed.

Before you begin actual construction, be sure to obtain the necessary permits from the local building department. Most communities require copies of your proposed design, along with a standard form to be filled out. Once you have submitted the application and paid the fee, a building inspector will review your proposed construction. Any changes required by local

codes will be indicated. When approved, you will receive a building permit for a specified construction period, which varies in duration in various locales. You must complete construction within that period, although you can apply for an extension, which is usually granted. During the work period, an inspector may examine the the deck construction. Normally, the inspector will examine the foundation before it is covered and conduct a final inspection before issuing an occupancy permit. This procedure varies from one community to another, so check your local requirements.

Railings. Although railings are often considered decorative parts of a deck, building codes frequently dictate that they not only must be provided, but that they must measure a specified height. Railings can be attached to the decking or to the extended posts. Railings must be both stable and able to support a heavy load. People lean against them and furniture pushes against them. For this reason, the best design ties the railings in with the posts or beams.

Tools

You can build a deck with a modest set of tools (see page 26). For preparing the site you will need a shovel and pick. For mixing concrete you will need a wheelbarrow, hoe, and shovel; if you have a lot of footings to set, consider renting a canister-type cement mixer. For setting out the plan, have a tape measure, ruler, twine, pencil, plumb bob, level and framing square. To cut wood you will need a power circular saw, hand saw, and power jig saw. For assembling the parts, a power drill, hammer, screwdriver, wrenches for bolts and lag screws, nail set, and chisel are necessary. When finishing the surface, brushes, a pan, and a roller will be sufficient. Be sure you have the proper safety equipment: goggles and gloves.

Fasteners

All the structural elements of a deck discussed at the beginning of this chapter—from the decking down through the posts—are fastened together by nails, screws, bolts, and metal connectors (see page 27). Although it is possible to build a deck using only nails, screws, and bolts, you will have a more stable and longer-lasting deck if you use metal connectors, especially for joining posts, joists, ledgers, and other large structural members. The added cost is worth it in the long run. All fasteners and connectors that you use should be specifically intended for outdoor use, and must be rust-resistant.

Nails. Use galvanized nails; they are available everywhere and will not rust as long as the zinc coating is not broken. They can be used for all parts of your deck construction. There are two other types of nails that resist rust. Aluminum nails resist rust better than galvanized nails, but they are not as strong and cost more. Stainless steel nails are available in some places; they resist rust best of all but are expensive. Nails are usually sold by the pound, either from open stock or in packages. The price depends on their material and coating, if any, the design, and the size (shown in penny sizes: 10d means ten-penny––the d denotes the old English pennyweight). Two important rules of thumb to remember: First, always use nails that are about twice as long as the thickness of the top piece of lumber you are nailing. For example, if you are putting down 2x4 decking, use 12d or 16d nails (the 2x4 is $1\frac{1}{2}$ inches thick; the nails are $3\frac{1}{4}$ and $3\frac{1}{2}$ inches long). Second, blunt the sharp points of nails with a hammer to prevent them from splitting the wood.

Types of Nails. Nails used in deck construction are shown on page 27; the most common types are described below.

Common nails and box nails are used to secure decking and other structural members. They have large, flat heads.

Finishing nails are used when an exposed nail head is undesirable. These small-headed nails are used on parts such as railings and seats. Spiral nails are used for plywood, roof coverings, and sometimes for decking lumber. These nails hold very well. Double-head nails have two heads so that they can be removed from temporary construction such as braces and forms.

Special-purpose nails such as concrete nails, joist-hanger nails, and fiberglass panel nails are made for the limited uses indicated by their names.

Screws and Bolts. These fasteners are more expensive than nails and take longer to install but the resulting connection is stronger. They are recommended for railings, stairs, benches and other constructions that must resist a great deal of pressure against the connection.

Using Screws. The threaded part of the wood screw should reach completely into the second piece of wood. First drill pilot holes to prevent the wood from splitting. A screw-pilot bit in a power drill produces both a pilot hole for the screw threads and a countersink hole for the screw head.

Deck screws are designed to be easily driven into the softwood typically used in deck construction. Drilling pilot hole and countersinking is not necessary with deck screws. A Phillips-head screwdriver tip mounted in a power drill speeds up construction.

Using Bolts. Buy bolts that are one inch longer than the combined thickness of the pieces being joined. Drill a hole through the wood that is 1/16 inch larger than the bolt diameter.

Connectors

When used in conjunction with screws and nails, metal connectors add rigidity to a deck and ensure a stronger and longer-lasting connection (see page 27). They are available in preformed shapes intended for making specific joints, such as post to footing and joist to ledger. Use joist-hanger nails to make all the connections.

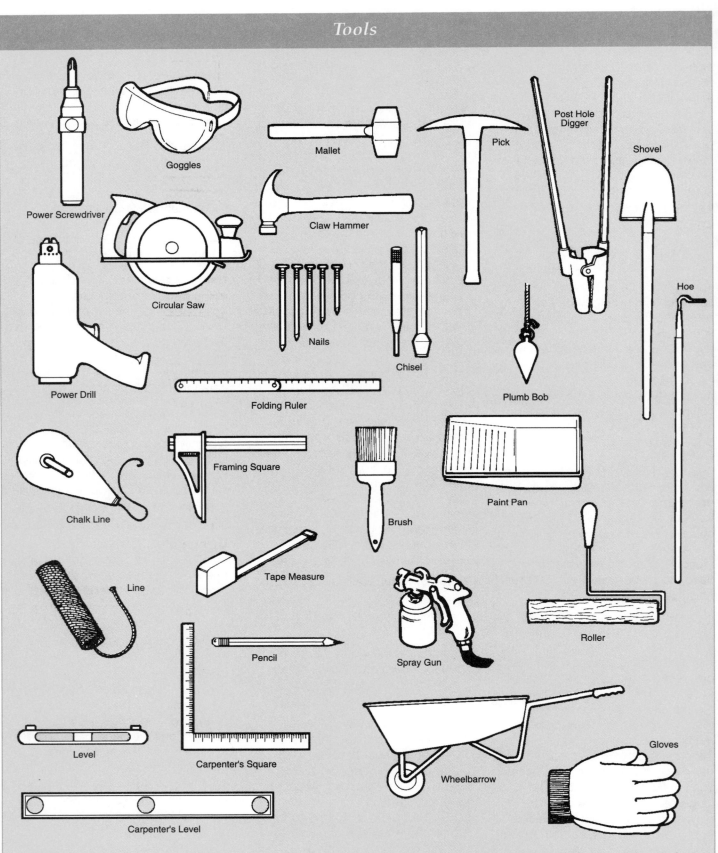

Power Screwdriver

Goggles

Mallet

Pick

Post Hole Digger

Shovel

Claw Hammer

Circular Saw

Power Drill

Nails

Chisel

Plumb Bob

Hoe

Folding Ruler

Chalk Line

Framing Square

Brush

Paint Pan

Line

Tape Measure

Roller

Pencil

Spray Gun

Level

Carpenter's Square

Wheelbarrow

Gloves

Carpenter's Level

The tools and equipment shown above are essential for preparing the site, cutting and assembling the parts, and maintaining the decks described in this book.

Fasteners

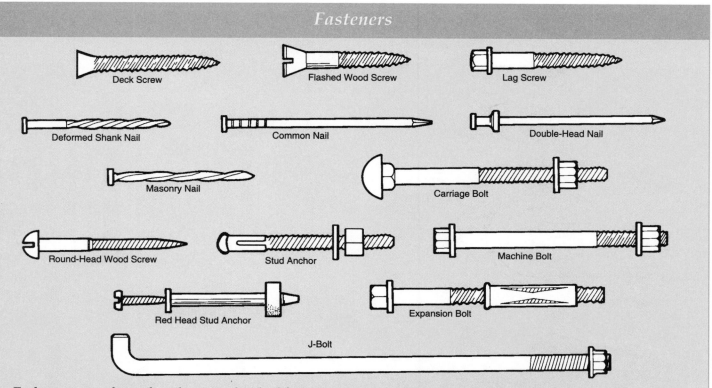

Deck Screw

Flashed Wood Screw

Lag Screw

Deformed Shank Nail

Common Nail

Double-Head Nail

Masonry Nail

Carriage Bolt

Round-Head Wood Screw

Stud Anchor

Machine Bolt

Red Head Stud Anchor

Expansion Bolt

J-Bolt

Each connector shown here has its individual function in deck construction; when used for that purpose (described in the text), it ensures a safe, reliable structure.

Connectors

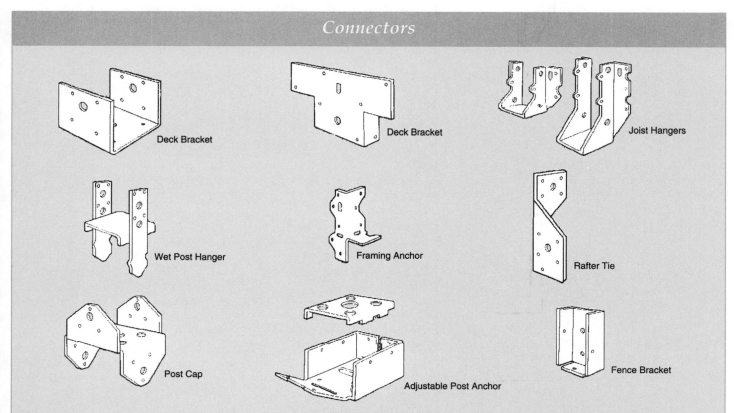

Deck Bracket

Deck Bracket

Joist Hangers

Wet Post Hanger

Framing Anchor

Rafter Tie

Post Cap

Adjustable Post Anchor

Fence Bracket

Use metal connectors and plates designed specifically for joining deck components; they provide the most stable and long-lasting decks.

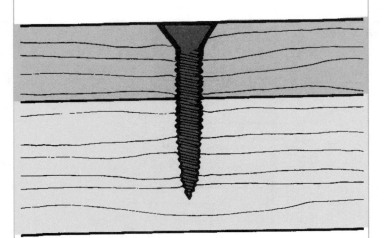

The threads of a screw should be completely sunk into the second piece of wood.

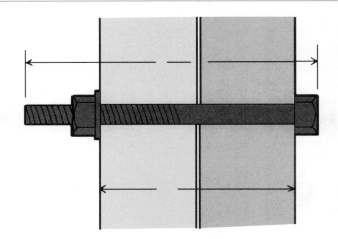

Blunt the ends of sharp nails with a hammer, to avoid splitting lumber. Drill pilot holes near ends of lumber.

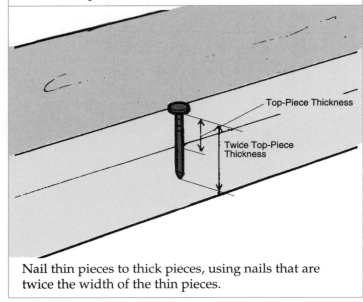

Nail thin pieces to thick pieces, using nails that are twice the width of the thin pieces.

Use bolts that are 1 in. longer than the total thickness of the boards being joined together.

Deck Finishes

It is a good idea to apply a finish to the exposed wood surfaces of your deck to protect it from the effects of weather and sun. If you want to see the grain, texture, and/or color of the wood, use a water-repellent, natural finish containing a wood preservative. There are three types of deck finishes: Clear, penetrating finishes delay that the effects of weathering but allows grain, texture, and color to remain visible. Semitransparent stains are easy to apply. They let the grain and texture of the wood show but modify the color. They might be useful, for example, if you want the deck to match the house.

Solid-color stain lets the wood texture show but masks the grain and the original color. Applied to badly weathered wood, a solid-color stain produces a durable, renewed finish. Generally, you should not use clear surfaced finishes, such as polyurethane or varnish that leave a surface film. The coating will break and deteriorate in time, hastening wood decay. If you want to cover the grain, texture, and color of the wood entirely, apply paint. Use an exterior oil-base or an exterior latex paint. A latex paint goes on easier than an oil-base paint; brushes, rollers, pans, and hands are easily cleaned in water. Oil-base paint provides stronger, longer-lasting protection, especially on weathered, rough, or previously painted wood, but turpentine or paint thinner is required for cleanup.

BUILD: FREESTANDING DECK

This chapter describes the construction of a simple, freestanding wood deck that is supported on posts and concrete footings. You can adjust these instructions to fit the variations of your own design. The purpose here is to provide you with many of the construction tips that professionals use in building a deck.

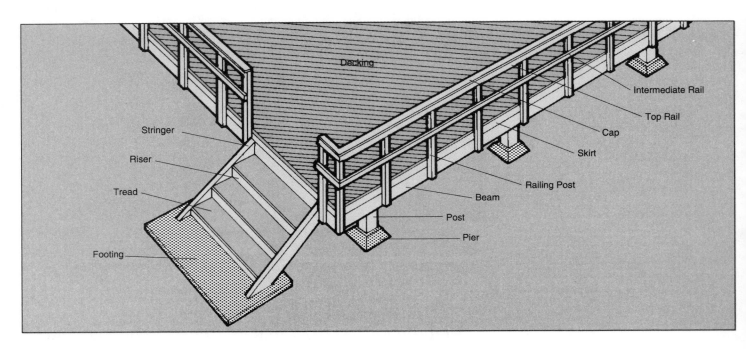

Decking — Intermediate Rail — Top Rail — Cap — Skirt — Railing Post — Beam — Post — Pier — Stringer — Riser — Tread — Footing

Materials List

8 x 8 DECK	
4	4 x 4 x (deck height) posts
4	2 x 6 x 8 headers
9	2 x 6 x 8 joists
18	2 x 6 deck boards
6lbs.	10d nails

8 x 12 DECK	
6	4 x 4 x (deck height) posts
4	2 x 6 x 12 headers
14	2 x 6 x 8 joists
18	2 x 6 deck boards
7 lbs.	10d nails

8 x 10 DECK	
4	4 x 4 x (deck height) posts
4	2 x 6 x 10 headers
11	2 x 6 x 8 joists
18	2 x 6 x 10 deck boards
6lbs.	10d galvanized nails

8 x 14 DECK	
6	4 x 4 x (deck height) posts
4	2 x 6 x 16 headers
16	2 x 6 x 8 joists
18	2 x 6 x 14 deck boards
8lbs.	10d galvanized nails

8 x 16 DECK	
6	4 x 4 x (deck height) posts
4	2 x 6 x 16 headers
16	2 x 6 x 8 joists
18	2 x 6 deck boards
9lbs.	10d galvanized nails

10 x 10 DECK	
4	4 x 4 x (deck height) posts
4	2 x 8 x 12 headers (cut)
11	2 x 8 x 12 joists
21	2 x 6 x 10 deck boards
8lbs.	10d galvanized nails

10 x 14 DECK	
4	4 x 4 x (deck height) posts
4	2 x 8 x 16 headers
16	2 x 8 x 10 joists
22	2 x 6 x 14 deck boards
10lbs.	10d galvanized nails

10 x 16 DECK	
6	4 x 4 x (deck height) posts
4	2 x 8 x 16 headers
16	2 x 8 x 10 joists
22	2 x 6 deck boards
10lbs.	10d galvanized nails

12 x 12 DECK	
6	4 x 4 x (deck height) posts
4	2 x 8 x 12 headers
14	2 x 8 x 12 joists
27	2 x 6 deck boards
10lbs.	10d galvanized nails

12 x 16 DECK	
8	4 x 4 x (deck height) posts
4	2 x 8 x 16 headers
6	2 x 8 x 12 headers (cut)
19	2 x 8 x 12 joists
27	2 x 6 deck boards
15lbs.	10d galvanized nails

Structural Plan

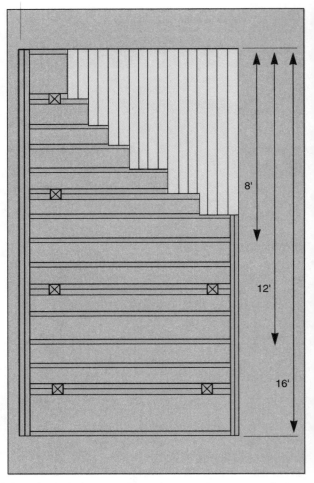

The materials lists and structural plan above will assist you in determining the relative number of posts, beams and joists needed for many different sized freestanding decks.

1. Before you order the building materials, clear the construction area. Remove all shrubs, rocks, and other obstacles that are not part of your design. Remove all wood since it will attract termites. Strip away grass and other ground cover.

2. Make sure the ground slopes away from the deck to ensure proper drainage. Build up the soil at one side of the deck or in the center if necessary, and slope it away from the high point to make positive drainage. Standing water can develop dank odors as well as provide a breeding place for insects. A slope of 1/8 inch per foot is enough to prevent accumulation.

3. If any roof gutters empty into or near the deck area, angle the downspouts to direct the runoff away from the deck. If that is not practical, install an underground line to drain water away from the deck to a dry well to a lower area. Check local codes for dry-well restrictions. Dig a $1^{1}/_{2}$-foot-deep trench that slopes from the downspout outlet down to the well, which should be about 2 feet wide and 2 or 3 feet deep. Fill the well with small stones. Run a line of 4-inch-diameter drainage tile in the trench, from outlet to well; cover the tile joints with roofing felt and 8 to 10 inches of gravel. Top the trench and dry well with a layer of dirt. The fill will settle over time, so pile it a few inches above the adjoining ground level.

4. After the footings are in place, cover the ground with a 4- or 6-mil-thick black polyethylene sheet and cover the sheet with 2 to 4 inches of gravel. This creates a maintenance-free area.

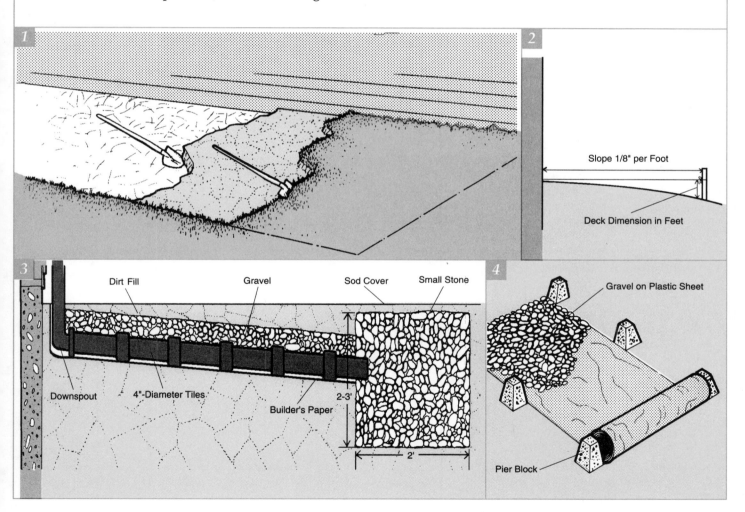

1

2

Slope 1/8" per Foot

Deck Dimension in Feet

3

Dirt Fill   Gravel   Sod Cover   Small Stone

Downspout   4"-Diameter Tiles   2-3'

Builder's Paper

2'

4

Gravel on Plastic Sheet

Pier Block

1 **Staking Out the Deck.** Start by laying out the deck on the ground. Even a freestanding deck should be built parallel or at right angles to a nearby house. Choose one corner of the deck near the house, a wall face or other structure, and mark it by driving a stake into the cleared, evenly-sloping ground. Stake out the four corners of the deck, using the triangulation survey method described below to make all dimensions exact and all corners square.

2 **Setting Up Batter Boards.** Set up two batter boards, as shown here, about 1 foot outside the first stake. Drive a nail into the board that is at right angles to the structure to which you are orienting the deck, and from that nail run a line parallel to the structure across the stake. Measure the desired dimension of the deck along that line and drive another stake. Set up batter boards in the same way at that location.

3 **Measuring By Triangulation.** Now, measure along the line 3 feet from the first stake A, and drive another stake B. From the first stake A run a second line perpendicular to the first. Measure out 4 feet to locate point C. If this second line is exactly at a right angle to the first, the diagonal between the 4-foot point C and the 3-foot point B will be exactly 5 feet, and you have a right-angle triangle. If it is not 5 feet, move the point C left or right until the diagonal measures 5 feet, and stake that point.

The 3-4-5 method is good for small distances. For greater accuracy with deck dimensions longer than 8 feet, use multiples of 3-4-5 to lay out right angles: 9-12-15 or 12-16-20, or more. Batter boards also can be used to lay out other angles.

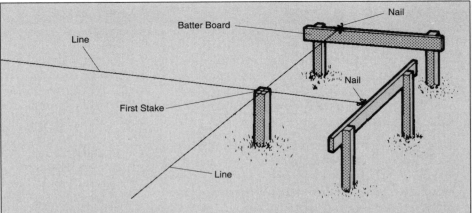

1 Construction begins with staking out your deck. Temporary batter boards set at right angles to each other mark the sides of the proposed deck and provide support for guide lines. A temporary stake at the intersection will mark the center of corner posts.

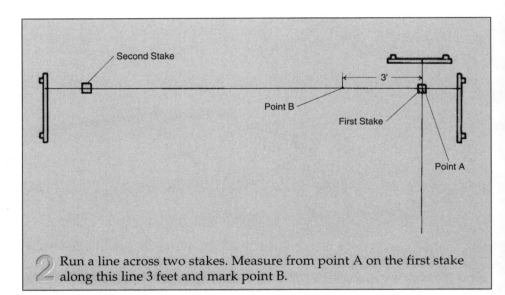

2 Run a line across two stakes. Measure from point A on the first stake along this line 3 feet and mark point B.

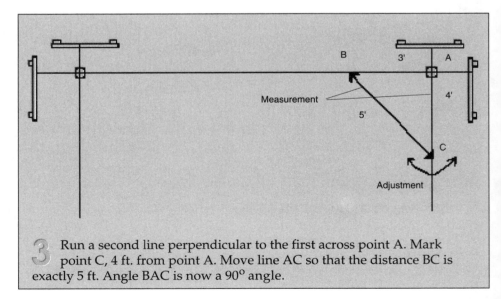

3 Run a second line perpendicular to the first across point A. Mark point C, 4 ft. from point A. Move line AC so that the distance BC is exactly 5 ft. Angle BAC is now a 90° angle.

Outlining the Deck. Stretch a line from stake A straight across C and fasten it to a temporary stake outside the intended deck area. Measure along this line from A and mark off the deck dimension in that direction. Drive a stake there and set up batter boards. Then use the 3-4-5 triangulation method to extend another line at right angles to the A-C line (it will run parallel to line A-B). Measure to the next corner and stake it. Continue until all corners of the deck area are connected by right-angle lines.

Check the accuracy of a square or rectangular deck layout by measuring the diagonals between opposite corners. If they are equal, all corners are right angles.

Locating Footing Holes. Once the deck corners are established, stake out the locations for the footings. Since the strings mark the outside dimensions of the deck, refer to the deck plans to see whether the posts are at the edge of the deck or set back 18 to 24 inches from the edge.

If the outside edges of the joists, beams and posts are to be in line, the point where the strings intersect marks the outside corner of the post. Use a plumb line to find this spot on the ground beneath the intersecting strings. Drive a stake into the ground inside this spot to mark the post center, until it is time to dig the hole.

If the outside posts are set back from the deck perimeter, set up lines parallel to the perimeter lines and locate the post positions with a ruler, plumb bob and stake. To find the positions of the posts inside the perimeter, follow techniques above.

Digging Footing Holes. A deck footing is a hole in the ground filled with concrete to which the deck posts are attached. It is best to mount the posts on concrete at least 6 inches above grade to prevent wood decay. The type of footing used dictates the size and depth of the hole to be dug (see pages 35-37).

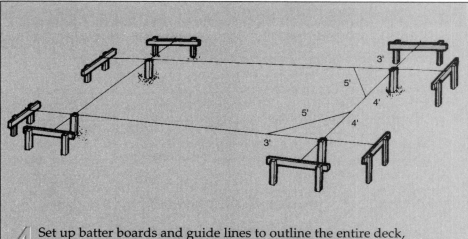

Set up batter boards and guide lines to outline the entire deck, making right angles at each corner using the 3-4-5 triangle method described in step 3.

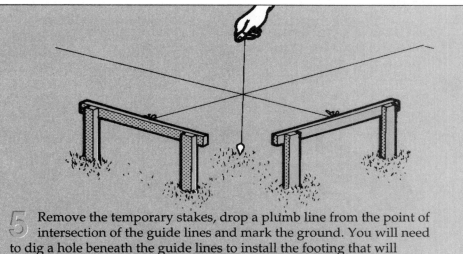

Remove the temporary stakes, drop a plumb line from the point of intersection of the guide lines and mark the ground. You will need to dig a hole beneath the guide lines to install the footing that will support the deck post.

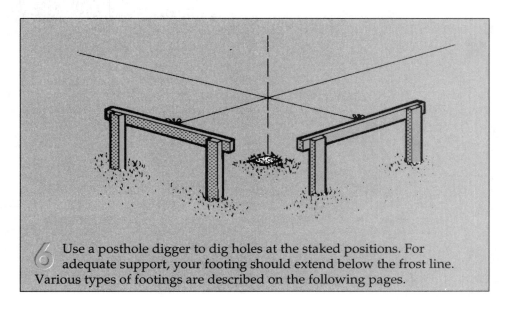

Use a posthole digger to dig holes at the staked positions. For adequate support, your footing should extend below the frost line. Various types of footings are described on the following pages.

The decision of whether to mix your own concrete or to have it delivered by truck, ready to pour, depends on how many footings you need and whether you would rather spend time and effort on mixing or money on premixed concrete.

To make a few footings, the simplest method is to buy sacks of dry mix. One 90-pound sack will make 2/3 cubic foot of concrete, which equals one 12x12x8-inch footing, the standard size. (A 12x12x6-inch footing equals 1/2 cubic foot, and a 12x12x12-inch footing equals 1 cubic foot.)

1. You can mix up 3 or 4 cubic feet of concrete in a wheelbarrow. Dump in the required amount of dry mix and mix it up thoroughly with a shovel or hoe. You will need about 4 gallons of water for 3 cubic feet and 5 gallons for 4 cubic feet.

2. Scoop out a hollow in the middle of the dry mix and pour in about half of the water.

3. Mix everything thoroughly. Add the remaining water a little at a time and mix constantly. Do not let any dry material accumulate.

4. Watch the consistency of the concrete carefully. Wet concrete should be stiff and it should mound up easily into a stable cone; it should not be sloshing around, nor should it be dry and crumbly. When a batch is ready, pour the footings immediately. If you are using precast piers or masonry blocks on top of fresh concrete, put them in place immediately and align them. Insert metal connectors into the concrete at once, and make sure they are level and aligned. Before using premixed concrete, estimate the amount you will need. Do not forget to include stair footings. Premixed concrete is usually sold by the cubic yard, which is 27 cubic feet. Call your supplier to find out what quantity he will deliver and at what price. Be ready to pour the footings when the truck pulls up; have a wheelbarrow handy.

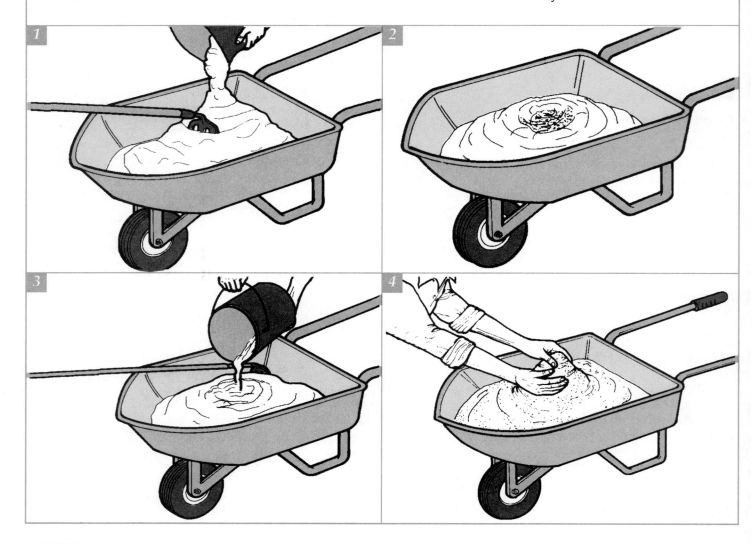

7 **Installing Footings.** The most effective footing for your design depends on the nature of the soil. Choose the best one for your situation. A pier block, which rests on the ground, is the most simple type of footing. Others are more complex, such as custom-made wood forms, mass-form concrete footings and ready-made concrete tube forms.

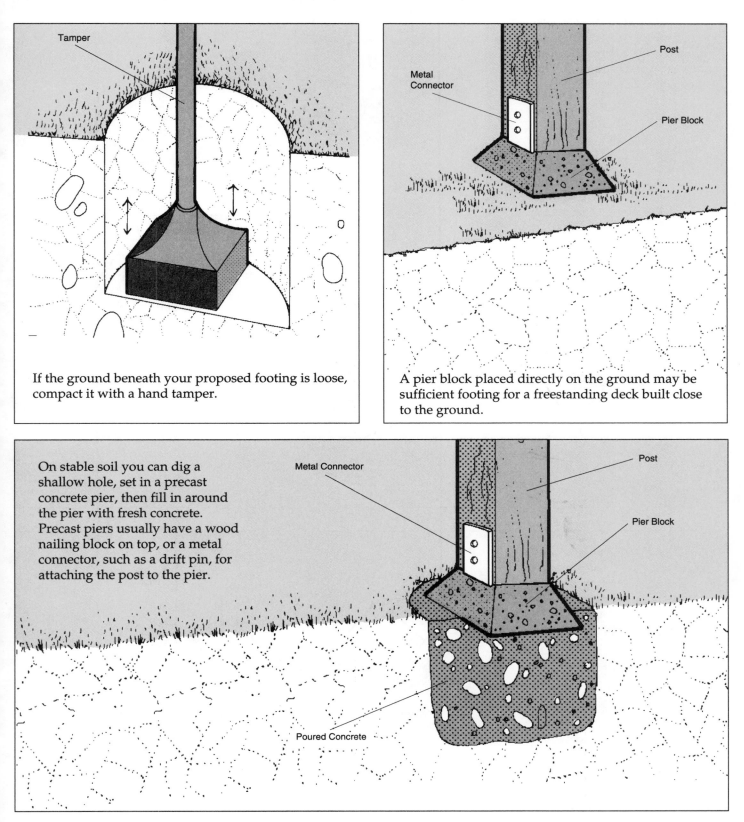

Tamper

If the ground beneath your proposed footing is loose, compact it with a hand tamper.

Metal Connector

Post

Pier Block

A pier block placed directly on the ground may be sufficient footing for a freestanding deck built close to the ground.

On stable soil you can dig a shallow hole, set in a precast concrete pier, then fill in around the pier with fresh concrete. Precast piers usually have a wood nailing block on top, or a metal connector, such as a drift pin, for attaching the post to the pier.

Metal Connector

Post

Pier Block

Poured Concrete

In firm ground, dig a 12x12x8-inch hole, fill it with concrete, build up a small mound, and insert a metal post connector. Be sure the connector is vertical. In damp areas, use a post-to-footing connector that raises the post an inch or so off the footing. This allows the post end to dry.

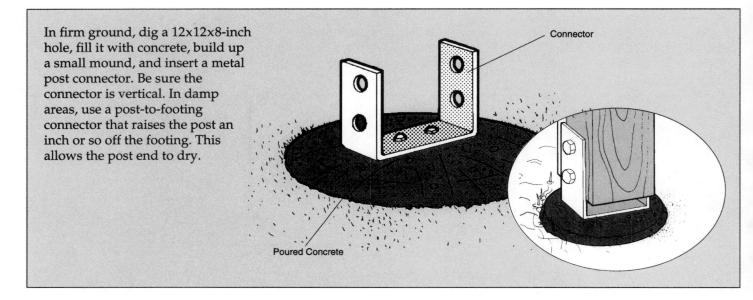

Connector

Poured Concrete

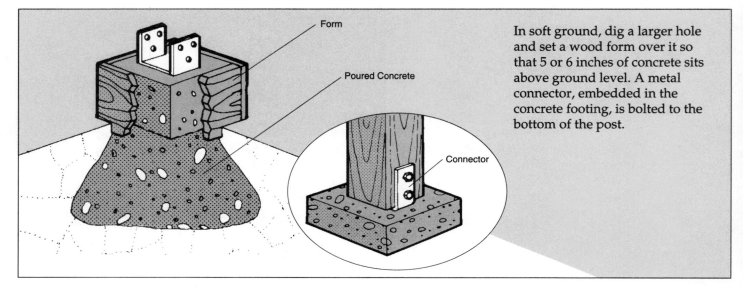

Form

Poured Concrete

Connector

In soft ground, dig a larger hole and set a wood form over it so that 5 or 6 inches of concrete sits above ground level. A metal connector, embedded in the concrete footing, is bolted to the bottom of the post.

If the soil is soft clay or a similar spongy material, use a mass-form concrete footing. This simple footing consists of a post embedded in a poured concrete foundation that is mounded up above the surface to shed water. An anchor strap is set into the concrete. The post should extend about 6 inches above grade. Use temporary braces to make sure the post remains vertical. Keep the braces in position until the concrete cures.

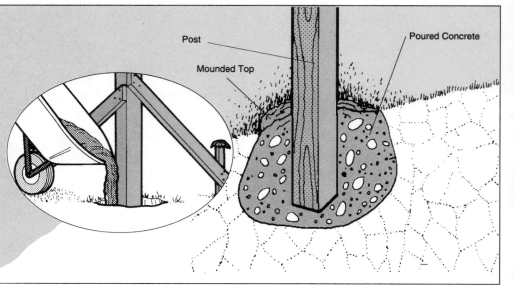

Post

Poured Concrete

Mounded Top

A ready-made concrete form is especially useful in sandy or gravel-like soils. It consists of a waxed-cardboard which keeps the surrounding soil from falling into the space where the concrete will be poured. This type of footing is available in a range of sizes.

The ready-made form is cut off a little above the desired level of concrete and placed in the post hole, which is somewhat oversized. Fill soil is then compacted around it to make sure that it is stable and will not shift.

The tube is braced using 2x4s fastened to the top. There are two ways to set the posts with a ready-made form. The preferred method is to fill the tube with concrete up to a few inches above grade, smooth it off, and insert a post strap or other metal connector into the concrete at the right level. Use a carpenter's level to make sure the connector is vertical.

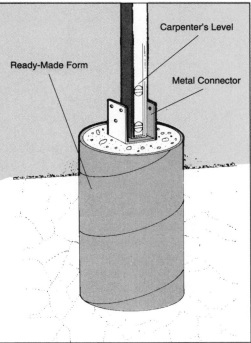

Another way to use the tubes is to insert the post in a larger diameter tube and then pour concrete around the post, making sure it is plumb and aligned with all other posts. A minimum tube diameter of 12 inches is recommended for 4x4 posts placed on top of the footing. A minimum tube diameter of 16 inches is recommended for a 4x4 post embedded in the tube. Brace the post with 2x4s set into the ground and aligned in two directions to make a right angle. If the inside of the tube is not treated to prevent the concrete from sticking, smear a little motor oil on the inner surface.

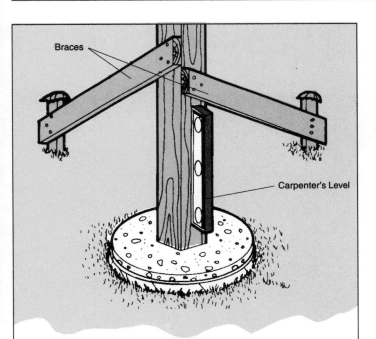

In northern climates where severe freezing occurs, the cement in the ready-made tube may crack unless it is reinforced with a steel rod. Insert a No. 5 size steel reinforcing rod in the tube, just short of the desired height. In areas that experience severe freezing, codes may specify that footings be placed below frost level, to avoid heaving that could damage the deck. After all the footings have been poured and the connectors put in place, wait three days and then remove the bracing, forms, and cardboard from the concrete.

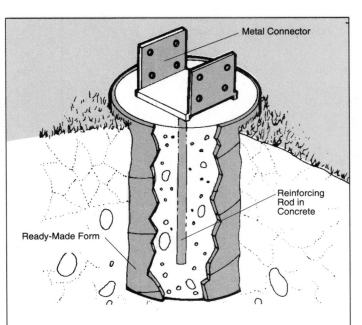

8 Attaching Posts to Footings.

When the concrete footings, piers and metal connectors have been installed, set up the posts. Use only pressure-treated lumber for posts, and for now cut them about 6 inches longer than their finished height. Later you can cut them down individually to accommodate differences in footing height once you have chosen one of the beam-attaching methods, explained below. Each post must be set plumb on its footing. All the hardware used to attach the posts to footings or piers should be high-quality, galvanized materials. The fasteners must anchor the post securely to the footing or pier (see pages 35, 36, 37). This is crucial in windy areas, for decks high off the ground, and for decks that support heavy weight. If you live in a wet climate, use a metal connector that raises the post end off the footing; this lets the post dry out, preventing decay.

A common way of connecting a post to a pier is to toenail the bottom of the post to a wood nailing block set in the pier. This is a weak method and is not recommended. If the nails rust out, the post could "walk" off the pier. Set up the posts in the connectors. Use two 2x4s set at a right angle to hold the posts vertical; check the posts twice to make sure they are both perpendicular and square to the lines of the beams they will support.

9 Setting Up the Beams.

There are two ways to attach beams to posts. In Method 1, the beams are attached to and rest on the tops of the posts. In Method 2, the beams are attached to the sides of the posts; the tops of the beams and the tops of the posts are flush. These two methods are described in detail on this and the following page.

Setting Up Beams: Method 1

Attaching to Post Tops

If your design calls for the beams to rest on the post tops, calculate the post height this way:

1. Establish the deck height above grade, subtract the thickness of the decking, the depth of the joist if the joist sits on top of the beams, and the depth of the beam.

Mark the calculated height on a corner post as a reference point. From this point run a string line with a line level (or a straight 2x4 with a carpenter's level) out to the other posts and mark the heights.

2. Cut off the post tops, making sure each cut is level. Lay the beams across the tops of the posts, according to your plan.

3. Look along each beam to see if it bows up or down; if it does, turn the high side up. Check to see that each beam is level. If it is not, slip thin pieces of wood between beam and post to raise the low spots.

4. Install the metal connector you have chosen. Toenailing the beam to the post is not advised because the wood may split and the nails will not resist beam twisting.

5. If the beams you are using do not span the full length of your deck, you may have to splice two shorter beams together. Center the joint over the top of a post as shown below. Stagger multiple splices across the deck.

6. Now you can cut off the ends of the beams. Use a chalk line across the deck to make sure that all the ends will be cut off at the same point.

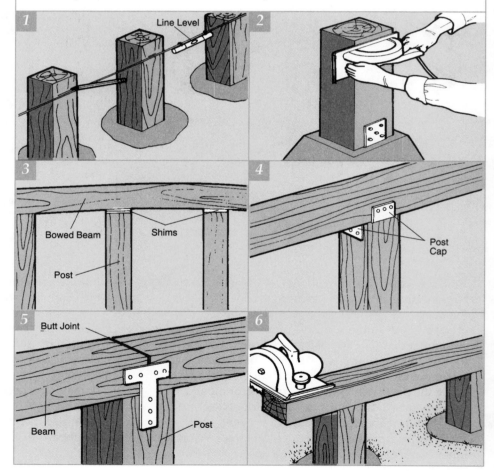

Attaching to Post Sides

1. If your plan calls for beams to be attached to the sides of the posts with lag screws, then the height of the posts is the height of the decking top minus the combined thickness of the decking and the joist depth, if the joists sit on the beam (see below).

2. Establish the desired decking height at one corner and calculate the height of that post; mark it clearly on the post as a reference point. Tack-nail one beam to each post in its row. (Partially drive two or three nails to make a temporary connection.)

3. Start at the corner reference point and make sure the beam is straight and level as you tacknail. Attach the

rest of the beams in the same way, leveling them to the first beam.

4. Then lay a straight 2x4 and a level diagonally across the beams to check that everything is level.

5. Now attach the beams permanently to the posts with 1/4x3-inch galvanized lag screws. Use at least two and preferably four at each connection. Drill holes as described on page 25.

6. When all the beams are attached, cut the tops of the posts flush with the beams (unless the posts must extend up to support railings or roof structures).

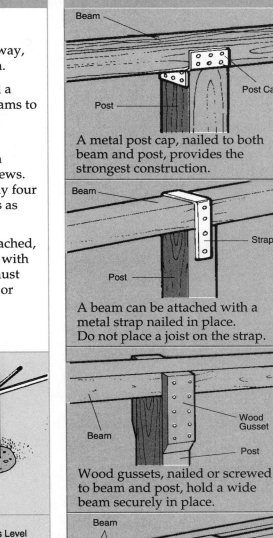

A metal post cap, nailed to both beam and post, provides the strongest construction.

A beam can be attached with a metal strap nailed in place. Do not place a joist on the strap.

Wood gussets, nailed or screwed to beam and post, hold a wide beam securely in place.

A double beam, made of two thinner pieces, sits in notches cut in the post top, held by bolts.

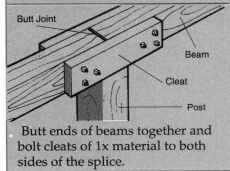

Butt ends of beams together and bolt cleats of 1x material to both sides of the splice.

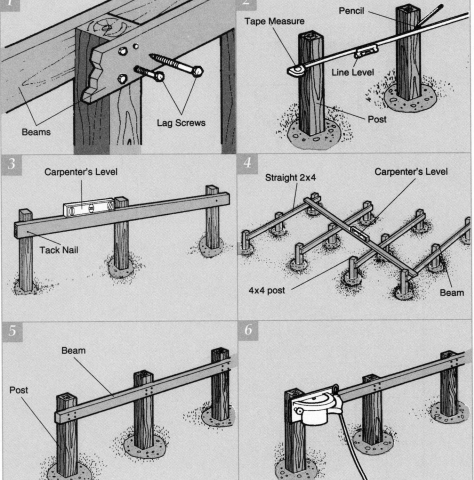

10 **Installing the Joists.** Once the beams have been attached to the posts, you are ready to install the joists. Two common methods are described right—setting the joists on top of the beams, and hanging the joists between the beams.

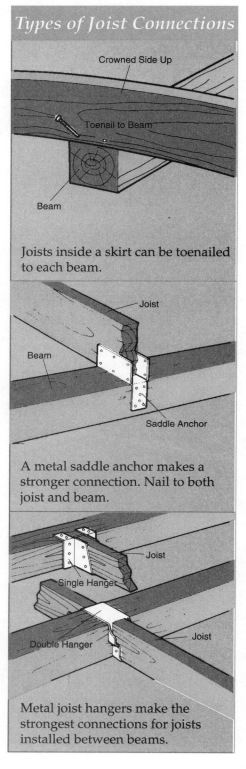

Types of Joist Connections

Crowned Side Up

Toenail to Beam

Beam

Joists inside a skirt can be toenailed to each beam.

Joist

Beam

Saddle Anchor

A metal saddle anchor makes a stronger connection. Nail to both joist and beam.

Joist

Single Hanger

Double Hanger

Joist

Metal joist hangers make the strongest connections for joists installed between beams.

Installing the Joists: Method 1

Joists Resting on Beams

1. If the joists rest on top of the beams, install the end or skirt joists first. The skirt is composed of the outside joists that span across the ends of the beams, plus the joists that cap the ends of all the other joists. First, carefully cut two skirt end joists to the design length. Then toenail them at the ends of the beams. Use two or three 16d galvanized nails for each connection.

2. Measure the distance from one skirt joist to the opposite one; then cut a cap joist to fit and install it. Do the same for the other cap joist. On the top edges of the cap joists, mark the complete joist pattern on 24-inch centers. Measure carefully between the cap joists and cut inside joists to fit.

3. To support standard decking, install joists at regular intervals between the cap joists. Start installing the inside joists at one side of the deck and work across to the other side, toenailing both ends of the joists to the beams and nailing through the face of the cap joists into the ends of inside joists. As you lay each joist in position, check if it is bowed; always turn the high side up. Toenail the joist to all inside beams.

4. Use a carpenter's square to make sure each joist is installed at right angles to the cap joists. Do not be concerned if the last two joists have a little more or less than 24 inches between them.

Another way to attach the joists to the tops of the beams is with beam saddle anchors; metal connectors that are nailed to both joist and beam.

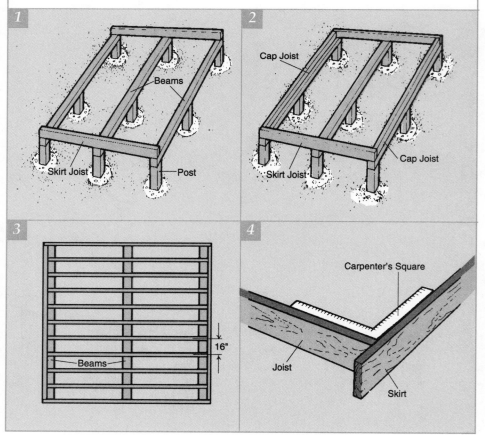

1
Beams
Skirt Joist
Post

2
Cap Joist
Skirt Joist
Cap Joist

3
16"
Beams

4
Carpenter's Square
Joist
Skirt

Joists Attached to Beam Sides

If the joists hang down between the beams, you have a choice of connection methods. One is the combination cleat and angle iron connetion. This requires cutting a wood cleat to size, then installing it with two metal pieces. The other metal connectors shown here are all one piece and can be attached more quickly. The double joist hanger is useful for attaching joists to inside beams; it lines up two joists automatically. For making connections to outside beams, you can use a single hanger (which also has a metal piece that sits on top of the beam), or one of the several anchor designs that are attached only to the side of the beam. Use 16d galvanized joist-hanger nails. Whatever connector you use, start at one side of the deck and mark the joist location on the ends of the outside beams.

1. If there are inside beams, snap a chalk line between the marks on the outside beams to mark the joist locations on the inside beams.

2. Space the inside connectors so that the joists are 24 inches on center. Use 10d or 12d nails.

3. Before you nail in a connector completely, use a framing square to check that both ends of the joist are exactly square to the beams.

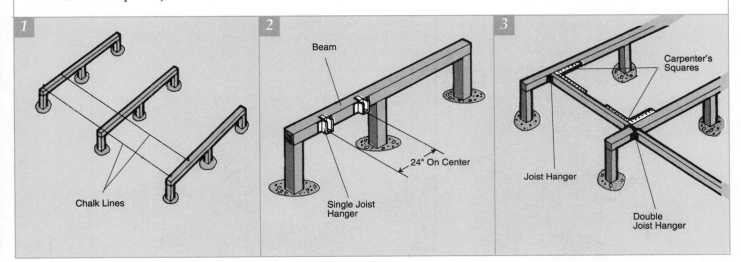

Joist Layout for Deck Variations

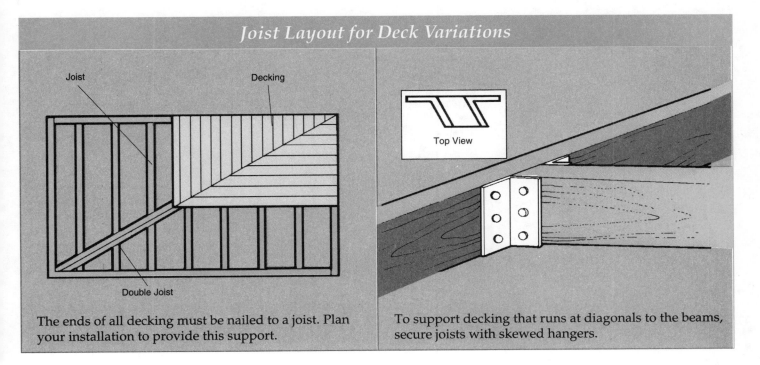

The ends of all decking must be nailed to a joist. Plan your installation to provide this support.

To support decking that runs at diagonals to the beams, secure joists with skewed hangers.

Splicing. If you cannot buy joists that extend the full length of your deck, splice two pieces together. Measure carefully so that the splice will be centered on top of a beam, and, if possible, centered over a post. Do not place adjacent splices over the same beam; stagger them across the deck. Two splices are shown below. One is made by overlapping the ends of two joists, so that they extend over the beam at least 6 inches. Drive 20d nails right through the splice and clinch the nail ends. You also can bolt or screw the joist ends together. Another way to splice joists is to butt them together and attach metal cleats on both sides. The cleats should cover more than half the width of the splice. Offset the nailing pattern in opposite cleats.

Blocking. If your joists are more than 8 feet long, brace them to prevent twisting, to stiffen the deck and to spread out the weight placed on it. The standard method of strengthening joists is to install blocking—pieces of lumber the same size as the joists that are nailed at right angles between the joists. This method is used for joists up to 2x10 size. Stagger the blocks so that you can nail them easily from the other side of the joist. Install blocking at intervals of 6 to 8 feet for a normal design with long, parallel pieces of decking. For other patterns place the blocking so that it will support the ends of short pieces of decking.

Bridging. If your joists are 2x10 or larger, wood or metal bridges are preferred to standard blocking. Bridges served the same function as blocking, to prevent twisting, stiffen the deck and distribute weight evenly. Both types of bridges use a pair of pieces in an X pattern. For wood bridges you must cut many small lengths of 1x4s or 2x4s, miter the ends, and toenail the pairs to the joists. Use at least two 6d or 7d nails at each connection. Although more expensive, metal bridges are easier and quicker to install.

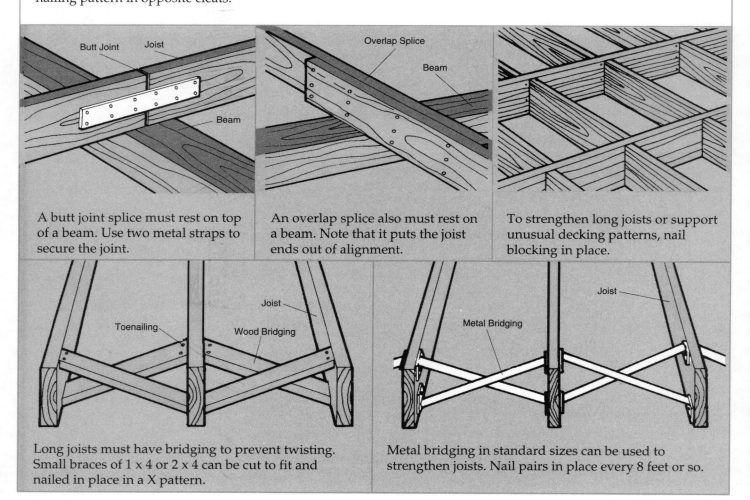

A butt joint splice must rest on top of a beam. Use two metal straps to secure the joint.

An overlap splice also must rest on a beam. Note that it puts the joist ends out of alignment.

To strengthen long joists or support unusual decking patterns, nail blocking in place.

Long joists must have bridging to prevent twisting. Small braces of 1 x 4 or 2 x 4 can be cut to fit and nailed in place in a X pattern.

Metal bridging in standard sizes can be used to strengthen joists. Nail pairs in place every 8 feet or so.

11 **Installing the Decking.** When the joists are in place and they have been braced, the decking can be installed. The most common type of decking used is 2x4s laid flat. The use of 2x2s and 2x6s also is common. As an alternate method, 2x4s can be set on edge.

Installing the Decking

1. Always lay the bark side of the board up. To do this, look at the end of the piece. The curve of the grain should point down. Use 10d nails or 3-inch decking screws set in a uniform pattern.

2. To begin, lay a chalk line across all the joists, and align the decking with it.

3. Drive nails or screws at an angle to anchor decking boards to joists. Use small nails as temporary spacers.

4. After putting down the first board, leave a space of 1/8 to 1/4 inch between succeeding boards to allow moisture to pass through and to speed the drying of the surface. Put scraps of wood or large nails between the boards to keep the spacing accurate. Getting all the boards parallel is difficult. Keep checking alignment.

If it is not exactly right, adjust the spacing gradually over the next two or three boards. When you are 6 feet or so from the end, put the last piece of decking down in line with the skirt and see how the remaining pieces fall into place. If in doubt, lay out all the boards before nailing or screwing them down.

5. If the deck boards do not reach the full deck width, cut them so that joints fall over a joist. Stagger the joints so they are not all on the same joist. The ends of every piece should be supported by a joist or by blocking.

6. After laying the decking, a nailset can be used to drive the nail heads below the surface of the boards. This is a finishing detail and is not absolutely necessary. If you do it, fill the holes with wood putty.

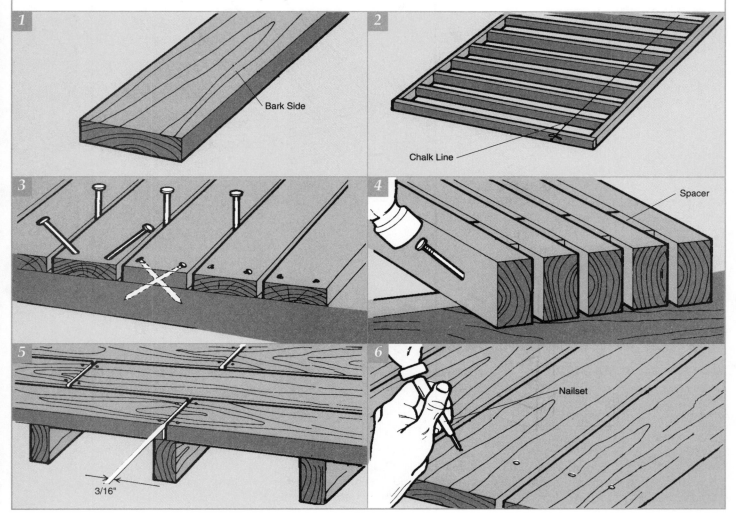

1 — Bark Side

2 — Chalk Line

3

4 — Spacer

5 — 3/16"

6 — Nailset

12 **Trimming the Decking.** The last major step is trimming the decking. Before you trim, verify all of the dimensions and make sure that things are square. Small discrepancies can be absorbed in trimming. Use a chalk line to mark the cut line. Use a power saw to cut the board ends and keep it away from the skirt or joist to avoid marring the surface. Apply a coat of wood preservative to the cut ends of all the deck boards. To cap the cut ends of the decking, as well as to provide an attractive edging strip, attach pieces of 1x3 or 2x3 across them. Try to use pieces long enough to avoid splicing, and nail them into each piece of decking so that no end can creep up over time (see below).

Cut off the protruding ends of decking pieces with a saw. Tacknail a guide board in place.

Nail long facing strips of thin lumber as edge molding to conceal the ends of the decking.

A Stepped-Deck Design

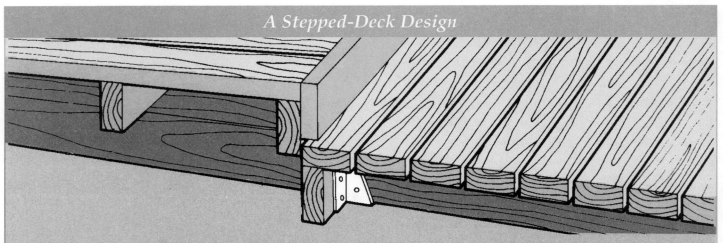

To join two deck levels with a moderate-height step, hang the lower joists to a cross beam attached to the upper level beam ends. The lower decking lies at right angles to the upper.

Boxing a Tree

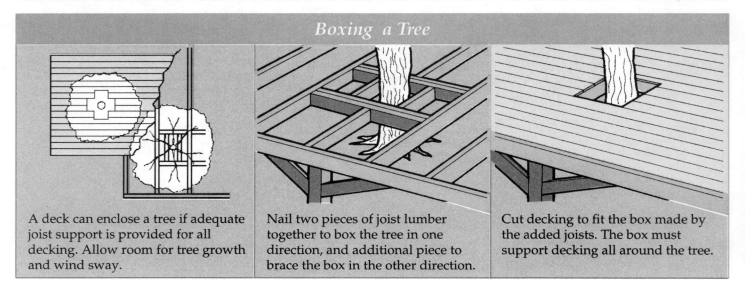

A deck can enclose a tree if adequate joist support is provided for all decking. Allow room for tree growth and wind sway.

Nail two pieces of joist lumber together to box the tree in one direction, and additional piece to brace the box in the other direction.

Cut decking to fit the box made by the added joists. The box must support decking all around the tree.

BUILD: ATTACHED DECK

Attaching a wood deck to your house or another structure can save time and money; when the house supports one end of the deck, you eliminate posts and beams along one side of the deck. In addition, this connection ensures that the house and deck will work together over the years.

1 **Planning the Deck.** If your deck is to be built over an existing set of concrete steps, you may leave the top of the steps as an entry space just outside the door or cover the stairs completely with the decking. Both options are illustrated right. If the steps are wood, remove them completely, so that the joists of the new deck are all attached directly to the house itself.

2 **Site Preparation.** When your plan is complete and approved by local authorities, proceed with the site preparation, described on page 31.

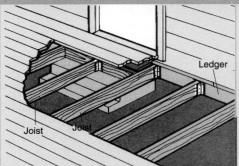
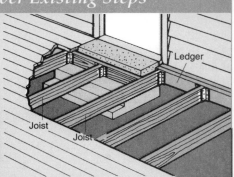

Building a Deck Over Existing Steps

If the top step is below the desired deck level, the decking can be laid continuously across the step as in a standard deck.

If the top step is at the desired level, the deck must be fitted around the step, with joist support provided on all sides.

Materials List

8 x 8 DECK	
1	2 x 8 x (deck width) ledger
4	4 x 4 x (deck height) posts
4	2 x 6 x 8 headers
9	2 x 6 x 8 joists
18	2 x 6 deck boards
6lbs.	10d nails

8 x 12 DECK	
1	2 x 10 x (deck width) ledger
6	4 x 4 x (deck height) posts
4	2 x 6 x 12 headers
14	2 x 6 x 8 joists
18	2 x 6 deck boards
7lbs.	10d nails

8 x 10 DECK	
1	2 x 10 x (deck width) ledger
4	4 x 4 x (deck height) posts
4	2 x 6 x 10 headers
11	2 x 6 x 8 joists
18	2 x 6 x 10 deck boards
6lbs.	10d galvanized nails

8 x 14 DECK	
1	2 x 10 x (deck width) ledger
6	4 x 4 x (deck height) posts
4	2 x 6 x 16 headers
1	6 2 x 6 x 8 joists
18	2 x 6 x 14 deck boards
8lbs.	10d galvanized nails

8 x 16 DECK	
1	2 x 10 x (deck width) ledger
6	4 x 4 x (deck height) posts
4	2 x 6 x 16 headers
16	2 x 6 x 8 joists
18	2 x 6 deck boards
9lbs.	10d galvanized nails

10 x 10 DECK	
1	2 x 10 x (deck width) ledger
4	4 x 4 x (deck height) posts
4	2 x 8 x 12 headers (cut)
11	2 x 8 x 12 joists
21	2 x 6 x 10 deck boards
8lbs.	10d galvanized nails

10 x 14 DECK	
1	2 x 10 x (deck width) ledger
4	4 x 4 x (deck height) posts
4	2 x 8 x 16 headers
16	2 x 8 x 10 joists
22	2 x 6 x 14 deck boards
10lbs.	10d galvanized nails

10 x 16 DECK	
1	12 x 10 x (deck width) ledger
6	4 x 4 x (deck height) posts
4	2 x 8 x 16 headers
16	2 x 8 x 10 joists
22	2 x 6 deck boards
10lbs.	10d galvanized nails

12 x 12 DECK	
1	2 x 10 x (deck width) ledger
6	4 x 4 x (deck height) posts
4	2 x 8 x 12 headers
14	2 x 8 x 12 joists
27	2 x 6 deck boards
10lbs.	10d galvanized nails

12 x 16 DECK	
1	2 x 10 x (deck width) ledger
8	4 x 4 x (deck height) posts
4	2 x 8 x 16 headers
6	2 x 8 x 12 headers (cut)
19	2 x 8 x 12 joists
27	2 x 6 deck boards
15lbs.	10d galvanized nails

Structural Plan

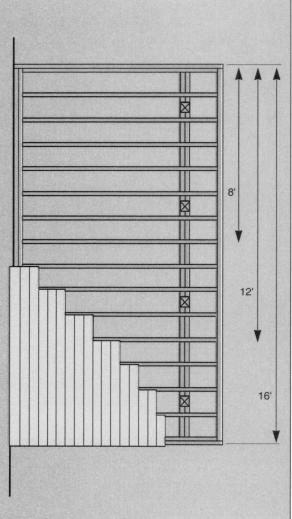

The materials lists and structural plan above will assist you in determining the relative number of posts, beams and joists needed for many different sized attached decks.

3 **Attaching the Ledger.** A deck is attached to a house by attaching a ledger (a piece of lumber the same size as the deck joists) and then connecting the deck joists to the ledger. Your local building code may specify the size, but for a deck about 75 square feet or larger, use a 2x8 or a 2x10. The deck joists can sit on top of the ledger or they can be attached level with the top, using metal joist hangers. If the house is brick or masonry, you can choose either method. If the house is wood construction, use joist hangers.

Parts of a Ledger Beam

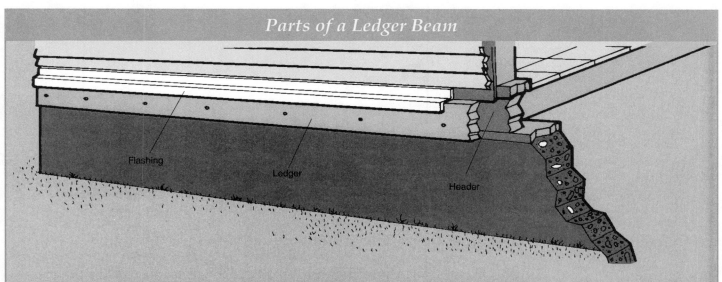

A wood ledger beam is bolted to the header joist (in a wood house), and a sheet of metal flashing is installed along the top edge to protect the ledger from moisture and decay.

Methods of Attaching Ledgers to Walls

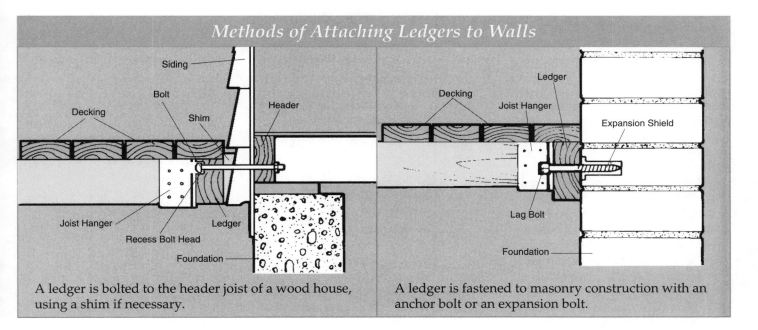

A ledger is bolted to the header joist of a wood house, using a shim if necessary.

A ledger is fastened to masonry construction with an anchor bolt or an expansion bolt.

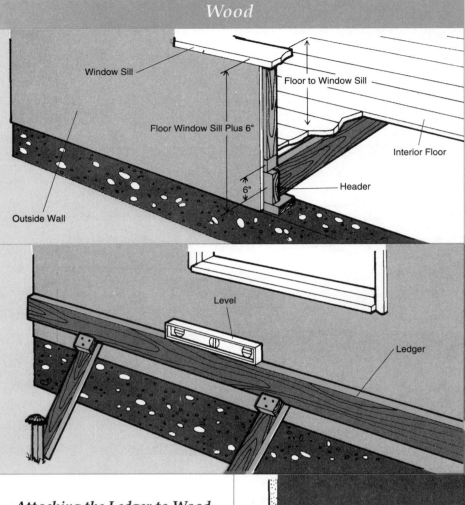

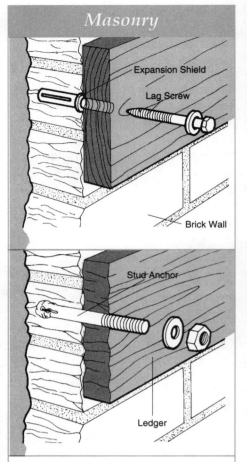

Attaching the Ledger to Wood.

The ledger should be securely fastened to the floor header, not to studs or to exterior siding. The header is exposed on some houses. If it is not, find the inside floor level at a door or by measuring down to the floor from an inside window sill and transfer that measurement to the outside wall. Measure down 6 inches more: this is the middle of the header. Brace the ledger up against the header or the mark. The top of the decking should be at least 1 inch below a door opening to keep water out. Place the top of the ledger 1 inch plus the thickness of the decking below the door. Tack-nail the ledger to the header and make sure it is level. Then install lag screws no more than 24 inches

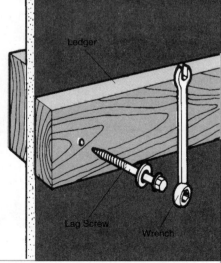

apart (use bolts if you can reach from the inside to add washers and nuts). Drill through the ledger into the header, and use a wrench to tighten the screws or bolts.

Attaching the Ledger to Masonry.

Hold the ledger up against the wall using temporary 2x4 braces with cleats. Use a wrench to drive the lag screws into the header, or to tighten lag bolts (top). Check that the ledger is level and drill holes through it no more than 24 inches apart; then use a masonry bit to drill holes into the wall. Remove the ledger and install expansion shields. Secure the ledger with lag bolts (middle). The ledger may also be attached by drilling the holes and driving stud anchors in place. Secure the ledger with washers and nuts (bottom). Check the level of the ledger again as you tighten bolts or screws with a wrench. If necessary, loosen the connectors and adjust the ledger.

4 Installing Protective Flashing.

If moisture collects between the ledger and the house, decay can result. If you live in a rainy area, prevent this by installing flashing, a strip of aluminum or galvanized metal shaped to lead water away from the joint.

To find the width of flashing you need, add the thickness of the decking to the width of the ledger, plus 1 inch. If the joists sit on top of the ledger, add their width.

Bend the flashing strips into the shapes shown at right, by clamping a strip between two 2x4s and carefully pounding out a right angle with a hammer and block of wood. To shape the flashing into the desired shape, clamp it between a pair of 2x4s and bend it with careful hammer blows (below). Preformed flashings also are available.

Depending on the type of siding found on the house, there are different ways to attach the flashing (see illustrations right and next page).

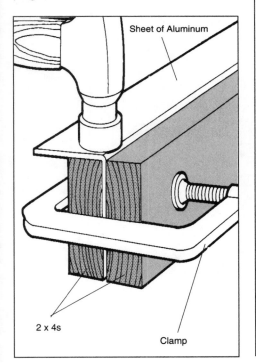

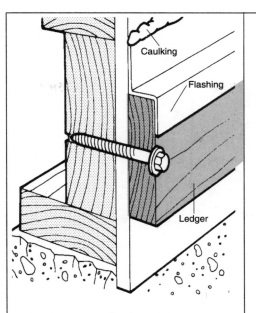

Flashing on Flush Siding. If the siding is flush, nail the flashing through it, into the wall studs, and seal the top with a bead of exterior grade or silicone caulking.

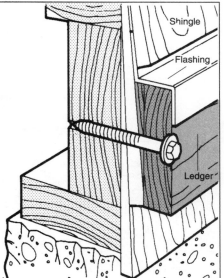

Flashing Under Shingles. If the house is shingled or has lap siding, slip the top edge of the flashing under the siding. Nail the flashing to the ledger and seal the joint with caulking.

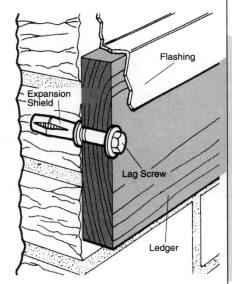

Flashing Over Masonry. If the deck is against masonry, fill gaps flush to the surface with caulking. Nail the flashing to the ledger top, or to the wall with masonry nails. Caulk top edge and nail heads.

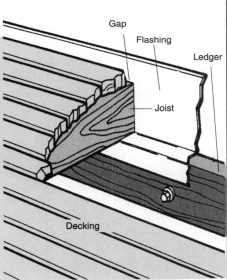

Flashing Behind Joists. If the deck joists sit on top of the ledger beams, be sure to cut the flashing wide enough to reach up above the joist tops. Attach flashing and caulk top edge and nail heads.

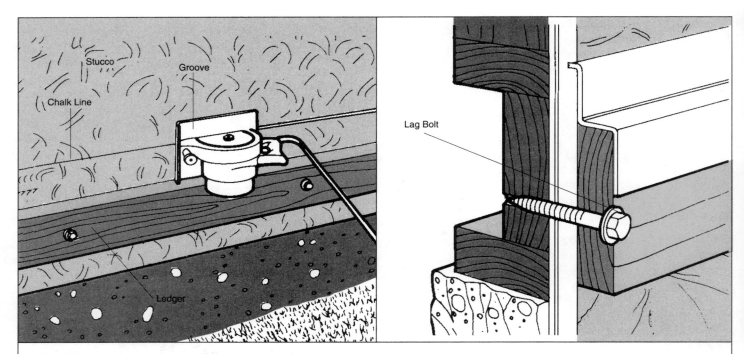

Flashing Over Stucco. If the house is stucco, mark a line just below the top of the decking. Cut a slot 3/8 in. deep in the stucco an inch or two above the ledger, using a circular saw with a masonry (carborundum) blade (left). Bend the top edge of the flashing strip to fit the slot. Nail the flashing to the ledger and caulk the joint at the stucco (right).

Alternative to Flashing

A simpler way to prevent water damage to the ledger is to install five or six metal washers on each mounting lag screw or bolt, between the house and the header. This provides enough air space for water to run down freely, without getting trapped, and for air to circulate to dry the wood surfaces. This eliminates the need for flashing. Care should be taken to maintain that the space remain clear of any debris that would clog the space and block the flow of water.

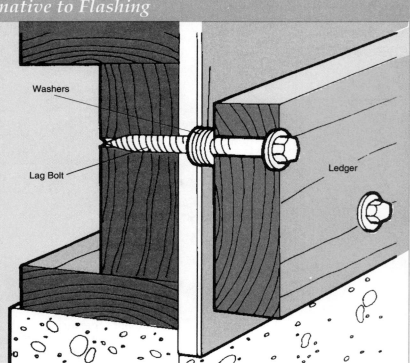

5 **Installing Footings, Posts, and Beams.** The first steps in building the supporting framework of an attached deck are like those described in detail on pages 37-43. They are summarized here. Locate the positions of the posts by setting up batter boards and running lines to mark the dimensions of the deck. Use the 3-4-5 triangle method to make sure the corners are right angles. Make the footings and set up the posts. Attach the beams. Be sure the beam tops are progressively lower than the ledger, working outward from the house, so the deck will slope slightly away for good drainage (top).

When the interior floor level is between 12 and 25 inches above ground level, the beams can rest directly on the footings; posts are not needed. The diagram at right shows how to do this (middle).

6 **Attaching Joists to Ledger.** If your joists rest on top of the ledger and beams, they may be attached by toenailing or by using a saddle anchor or hurricane anchor to make a secure connection (below left).

To install joist tops at the same level as the beam and ledger tops, use joist hangers to secure the joists in place (see page 40-41).

If your joists are more than 8 feet long, add bracing, as described on page 42 (below right).

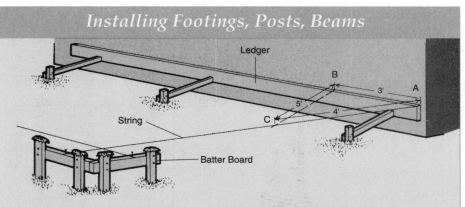

Installing Footings, Posts, Beams

Batter boards support strings that mark the position of deck posts. A string can be run at right angles to the house by setting up a triangle with 3-, 4- and 5-ft. sides.

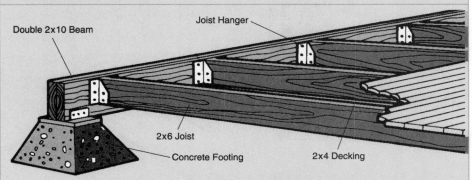

If posts are not needed, place the beams directly on the footings, securing them with metal connectors. The beams can be single pieces or doubled joist lumber.

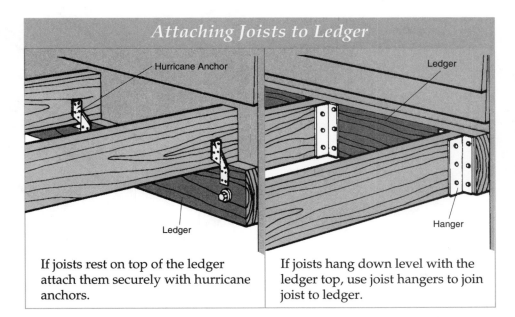

Attaching Joists to Ledger

If joists rest on top of the ledger attach them securely with hurricane anchors.

If joists hang down level with the ledger top, use joist hangers to join joist to ledger.

7 **Installing the Decking.** Decking patterns are described on pages 12 and 23; nailing techniques are explained on page 43. Decking should be installed parallel to the house. Allow a 1/2-inch gap between the house wall and the first piece of decking. Trim the outer edges of the decking as described on page 44.

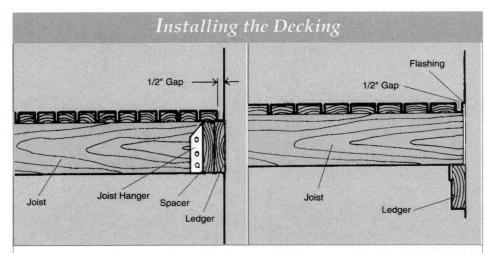

Installing the Decking

Whether the joists hang down level with the joist top or are mounted on top of the ledger, leave a 1/2-inch gap between the wall and the decking.

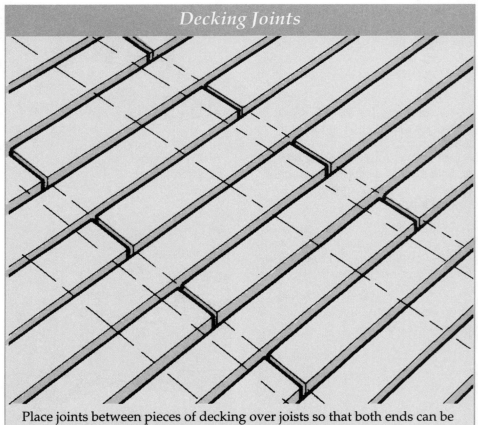

Decking Joints

Place joints between pieces of decking over joists so that both ends can be nailed down. Stagger joints across neighboring joists.

BUILD: RAISED DECK

A wood deck can be built up to about 12 feet above grade using the designs and construction techniques explained in this chapter. Check local building codes for limitations and support requirements. If you plan a deck higher than 12 feet, consult an architect or contractor.

Attaching Deck to Second Story

1 Installing the Ledger. Attach a ledger beam (2x8 or 2x10) to the second-story header, as described on pages 47-48. Level it and use 1/4 x3½-inch lag screws no more than 24 inches apart.

2 Making the Joist Skirt. Cut two skirt joists to the required length and nail them to the ledger ends, using three 10d or 16d nails. Make a temporary support of 2x4s for the outside end of these joists. Slope the joists down from the ledger, 1/8 inch per foot. Cut and install the third skirt joist. Use a diagonal 2x4 to hold the completed skirt square.

3 Attaching the Joists. Install the remaining joists on 18- or 24-inch centers (see chart on page 13). You can hang the joists from a cleat nailed to the ledger and the outer skirt, or from metal hangers.

4 Hanging the Beam. Cut a 4x6 (or two joists nailed together) to fit the width of the deck; snap a chalk line across the underside of the joists at the desired beam location. The joists can overhang the beam one quarter of their length (see page 40). Attach the beam to each joist, including the skirt joists, with a metal connector.

5 Locating the Footing. Mark the post positions on the underside of the beam and drop a plumb line from each position to the ground to find the location of the footing holes. Mark these spots with stakes.

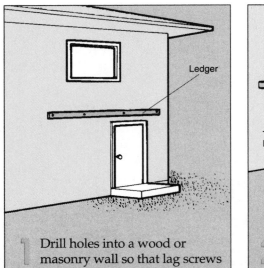
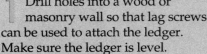

1 Drill holes into a wood or masonry wall so that lag screws can be used to attach the ledger. Make sure the ledger is level.

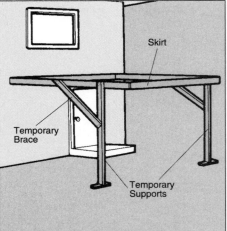

2 Two side skirt joists are attached to the ledger; temporary supports hold them up while the outside skirt joist is installed.

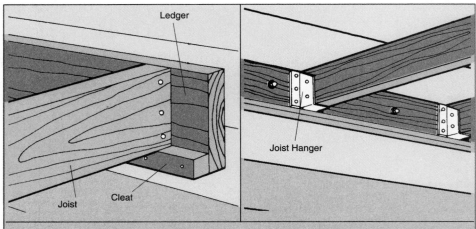

3 Joists can rest on wood cleats that are nailed or screwed to the bottom edge of the ledger; toenail the joists to the ledger (left). Joists also can be attached to the ledger with metal hangers (right).

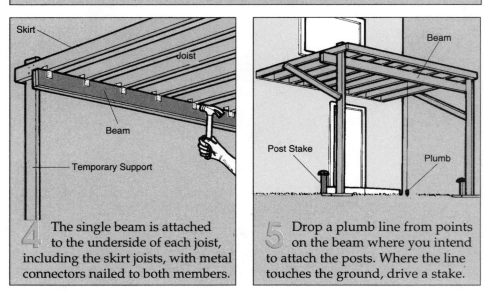

4 The single beam is attached to the underside of each joist, including the skirt joists, with metal connectors nailed to both members.

5 Drop a plumb line from points on the beam where you intend to attach the posts. Where the line touches the ground, drive a stake.

6 Digging the Footing Holes. Dig holes at each of the stakes (you can rent a posthole digger for this chore). The holes should be at least 24 inches deep; in areas of freezing and thawing the bottom should be 8 inches below the frost line. The holes should be 12 to 14 inches in diameter (check local codes).

7 Hanging and Bracing Posts. Cut the posts to reach down to the frost line; there should be 8 to 10 inches between the bottom of the post and the bottom of the hole. Coat all post ends with preservative. Attach the posts to the beams with metal connectors. Brace the posts with scraps of wood staked in the ground. Make sure the posts are vertical. (Exterior posts can be extended to support a railing; see page 62.)

Turn to page 57 for instruction.on "Bracing Posts of a Raised Deck."

8 Pouring the Footings. Mix up enough concrete to make the footings (see pages 34-37). Pour the concrete around the posts; be careful not to move the posts out of line. Mound the concrete up around the posts 2 or 3 inches above grade to provide drainage. Let the concrete cure for three days before removing the bracing.

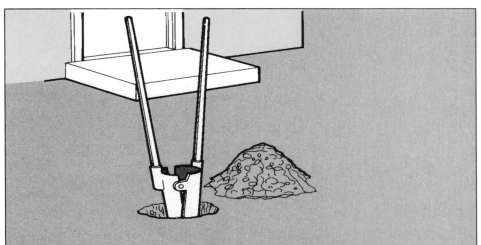

Use a posthole digger to dig holes at the staked positions. Follow local codes for the depth and diameter of the holes.

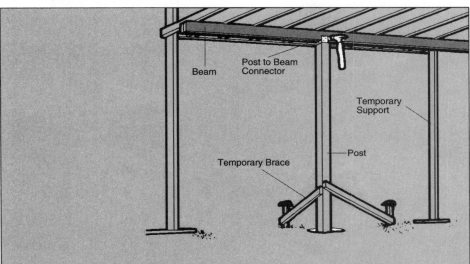

Beam
Post to Beam Connector
Temporary Support
Temporary Brace
Post

Hang the posts in the holes; attach to the beam with metal connectors. Support the posts with wood braces staked in the ground.

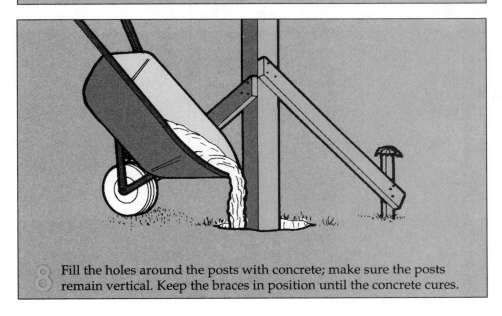

Fill the holes around the posts with concrete; make sure the posts remain vertical. Keep the braces in position until the concrete cures.

9 **Installing the Deck.** Nail down the decking parallel to the house, beginning at the house. Leave a 1-inch gap between decking and wall. Use a large nail or a scrap of wood to space the decking boards about 1/4 inch apart. Countersink the nail heads and fill the holes with putty (see page 43).

10 **Trimming the Deck.** When all the decking has been installed, snap a chalk line across the ends of the pieces at the desired place, or tack down a straight board as a saw guide. Trim the ends off along the line with a circular saw. Apply a coat of preservative to the newly cut ends.

9 Nail decking to joists, parallel to the house, with two nails into each joist. Start at the house, with a 1/2-in. gap to the first board.

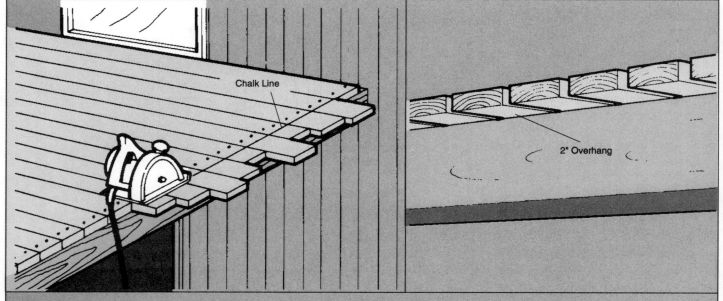

Chalk Line

2" Overhang

10 When all the decking has been installed, snap a chalk line across the ends of the pieces at the desired place, or tack down a straight board as a guide . Use a circular saw to trim the ends of the decking. Be careful to keep the saw blade away from the skirt joists (left). Decking boards can be trimmed flush with the skirt (as shown page 44) or you may want to leave a 2-in. overhang (right).

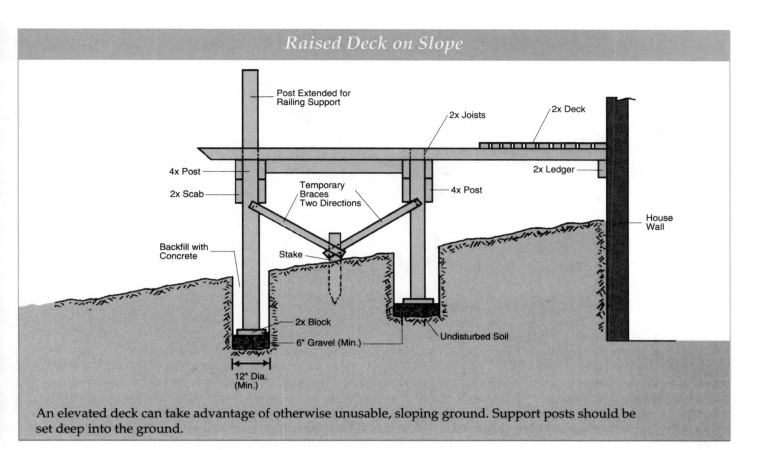

An elevated deck can take advantage of otherwise unusable, sloping ground. Support posts should be set deep into the ground.

Bracing Posts of a Raised Deck

If your deck stands more than 4 feet off the ground, the posts should be braced to provide stability.

If the deck is supported by only two posts and attached to a ledger beam, the posts should be braced to the joists. To brace the deck shown here, cut two pieces of 2x4 or 2x6 and attach them from the post to the inside of the skirt joist. The braces should be placed at a 45-degree angle, and the tops should be no more than 2 feet from the post. Cut the ends of the braces so that they stand vertical; this prevents moisture accumulation and the resulting wood decay. Cut the ends of the braces flush with post and joist. Use bolts or lag screws to install the braces. It may be necessary to insert blocking between the brace and the post and/or the joist.

If more than two posts support the deck, the braces should run from post to post. Bracing should be installed in a continuous pattern all around the deck so that all outside posts are connected. The K-pattern bracing shown at right is a strong design. You can install two braces extending across three posts in an X pattern if desired. Cut all brace ends vertically. Where two braces meet, leave a 1/2-inch space between them for air circulation. Install braces with lag screws or bolts.

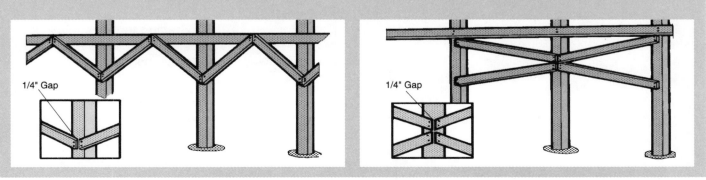

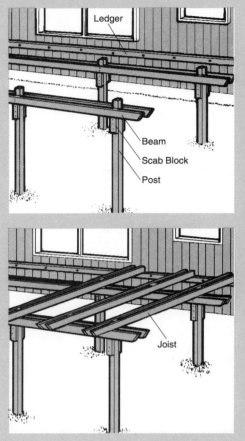

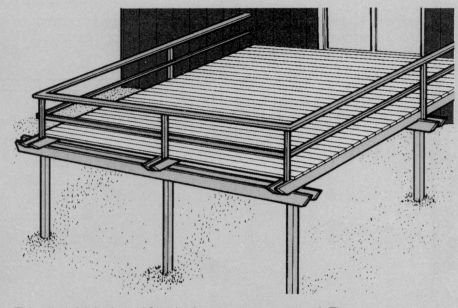

This deck is designed for sloping or uneven ground. The posts are installed first; beams and joists of doubled lumber are then attached to the sides of the posts. The posts can be extended up to support the railing, if desired. Screw or bolt scab blocks (beam support blocks) to each side of the posts so there is room above them for both beams and joists. Make sure beams are level. Rest joists on the ledger and on the beams at both sides of the posts. Screw or bolt the joists to the beams. Add the decking (see pages 43 and 44) and railings (see pages 61-64).

An Alternate Design

This variation is useful for a raised deck that requires two or more rows of posts, or one built on sloping or unstable ground. One side is attached to the house for stability.

1 **Installing the Ledger.** Attach the ledger securely (see pages 47-48). Be sure it is level.

2 **Setting Up the Posts.** Find the post hole locations as described on page 54-55. Dig down to stable ground, below the frost line if local codes require it. Put at least 6 inches of gravel in each hole. Cut 4x4 posts a few inches higher than the joist tops. Set the posts in the holes and brace them with scraps of wood. Fill with concrete and let cure for two days.

3 **Attaching Support Blocks.** Run lines from the ledger and mark the joist-top locations on the posts. Measure down from the marks a distance equal to the depth of the joists plus the depth of the beams, and mark a line for the tops of the support blocks. Attach blocks to both sides of all posts.

4 **Installing Beams and Joists.** Cut a pair of beams for each row of posts and enough joists for proper decking support (see chart on page 13). Rest the beams on the blocks and attach them to the posts with lag screws. Rest the joists on the beams. Attach them to the ledger with hangers, and to the posts with lag screws. Cut all inside post tops flush with joists.

5 **Installing the Decking.** Nail down the decking and trim the edges as described on page 44.

6 **Bracing the Posts.** Attach 2x4 or 2x6 bracing to all outside posts; see page 57.

BUILD: MODULAR PARQUET DECK

These instructions explain how to build a very simple deck directly on level, well-drained ground. This project shows how to build a 12x12-foot deck, using 3-foot parquet squares. It can be modified to fit other shapes and dimensions, still using modular squares.

Modular Decking

This type of deck is made up of 3-foot parquet squares. The result is a sturdy deck with an interesting pattern.

■ Materials List

32   2x4 3 ft. cleats
144 2x4 3 ft. decking
38 cubic feet of gravel
38 cubic feet of sand
about 8¼ lbs 10d nails
saw
hammer
shovel
soil tamper
rake

1 Making the Squares. Cut 176 pieces of 2x4 lumber, each 3 feet long. Sand off all rough edges. Use treated wood or heart cedar. Make a nailing jig out of scrap lumber, with inside dimensions of 36x36 inches. Place 3-foot lengths of 2x4s at opposite sides of the jig and nail nine 2x4 decking pieces to the cleats with two 10d nails at each end. Nail the first and last pieces in place to begin. Then space the remaining seven members equally. Repeat until you have 16 parquet squares (top).

2 Preparing the Site. Use the 3-4-5 triangulation method (page 41) to mark out the deck site. Remove soil within the site lines to a depth of 6 inches. Lay 3 inches of gravel on the bottom and level it with a rake. Spread 3 inches of sand over the gravel and tamp it down level (middle).

3 Placing the Squares. Lay the parquet squares in place, alternating the direction of the decking. Toenail them together. Fill the outside edge of the excavation with sand to ground level and tamp it down (bottom).

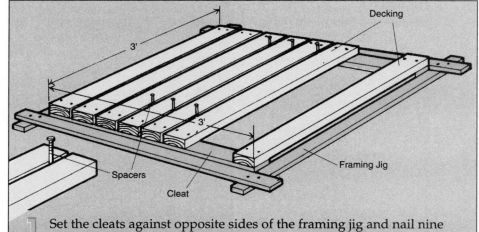

1 Set the cleats against opposite sides of the framing jig and nail nine decking pieces to the cleats so that they are evenly spaced across the module.

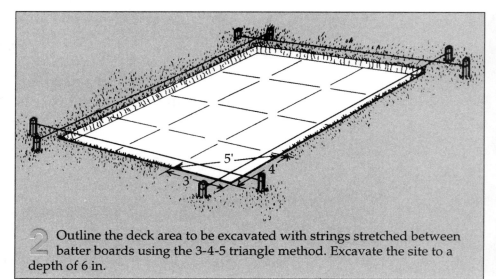

2 Outline the deck area to be excavated with strings stretched between batter boards using the 3-4-5 triangle method. Excavate the site to a depth of 6 in.

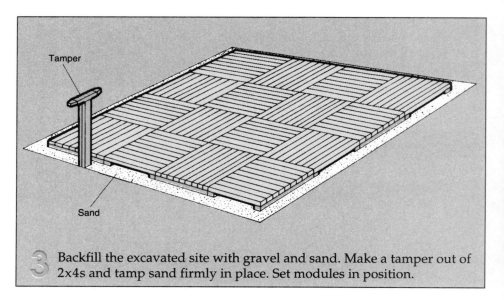

3 Backfill the excavated site with gravel and sand. Make a tamper out of 2x4s and tamp sand firmly in place. Set modules in position.

BUILD: DECK RAILINGS

Railings on a deck provide safety while adding a finishing touch to the deck. The varieties of railings are endless. In general, any deck that stands more than 24 inches above grade must have a railing. Check your local building code first. Railings usually must be 36 inches high and should have no openings larger than 9 or 10 inches square, to prevent small children from falling through. In any case, a railing must be strong enough to support people leaning on it.

Attaching Railing to Exterior Deck Posts

1 **Cutting the Posts.** If you want the posts that support the perimeter of the deck to support a railing also, use 4x4s long enough to extend the distance above the decking required by code. After the decking is installed cut off these posts at the railing height minus the cap board thickness (see Step 2).

2 **Installing Cap Boards.** The simplest cap is made of 2x4s screwed or nailed to the tops of the 4x4 posts. Center any splices directly over a post, using a butt joint. Miter two boards that join over a corner post. You can also use 2x6s as caps, with a reinforcing 2x4 beneath (middle).

3 **Attaching Horizontal Rails.** To strengthen the railing and fill in the open space, you can install 2x4s horizontally between the posts. Cut lengths to fit snugly and attach them with metal connectors, angle irons, or simple wood cleats. If more members are needed to make the railing sturdy or childproof, you can install additional 2x4s or 2x2s, either horizontally or vertically. Screw or bolt the fill-in pieces to the posts, or to the 2x4 cap boards and railings (bottom).

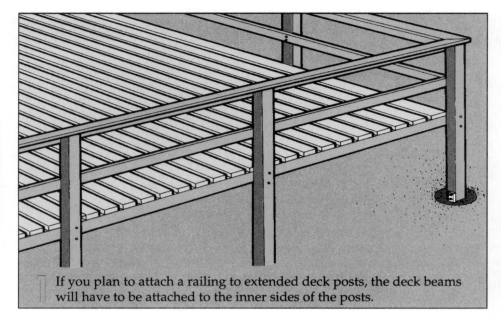

1 If you plan to attach a railing to extended deck posts, the deck beams will have to be attached to the inner sides of the posts.

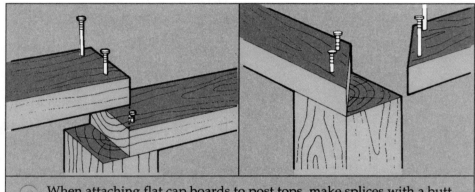

2 When attaching flat cap boards to post tops, make splices with a butt joint over the post (left). Attach ends of cap boards to a corner post top with a miter joint. Drill pilot holes for all nailing near ends (right).

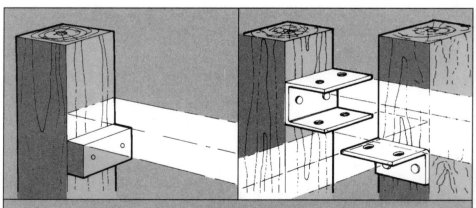

3 Horizontal rails may be supported on a wood cleat and toenailed to post and cleat (left). You also can attach rails to posts with metal connectors or angle irons for strong construction (right).

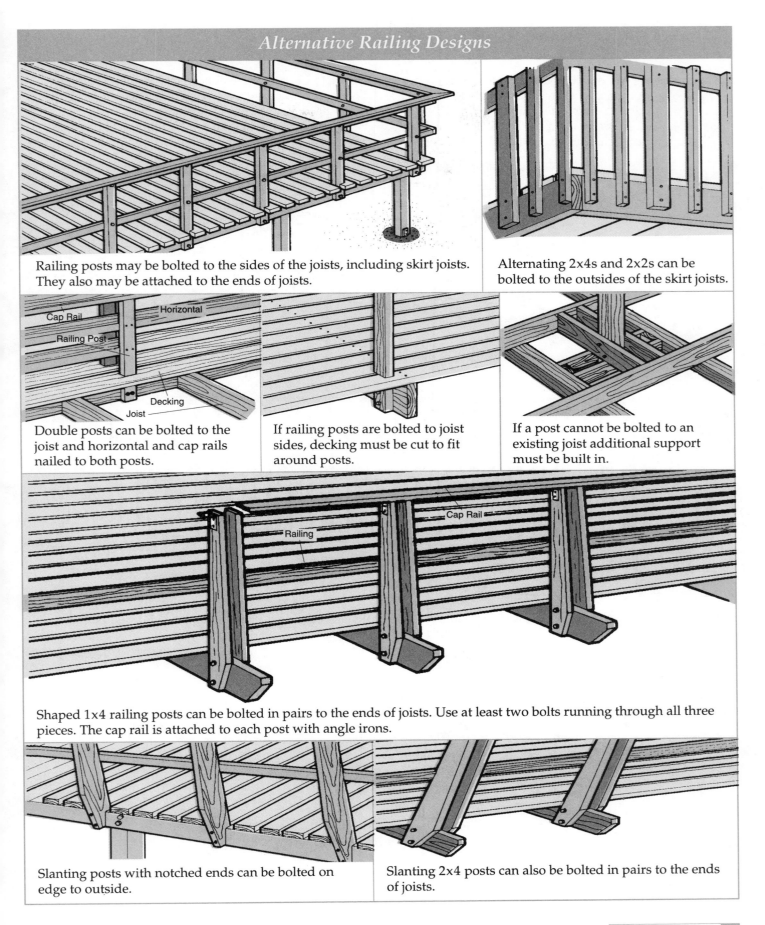

Alternative Railing Designs

Railing posts may be bolted to the sides of the joists, including skirt joists. They also may be attached to the ends of joists.

Alternating 2x4s and 2x2s can be bolted to the outsides of the skirt joists.

Double posts can be bolted to the joist and horizontal and cap rails nailed to both posts.

If railing posts are bolted to joist sides, decking must be cut to fit around posts.

If a post cannot be bolted to an existing joist additional support must be built in.

Shaped 1x4 railing posts can be bolted in pairs to the ends of joists. Use at least two bolts running through all three pieces. The cap rail is attached to each post with angle irons.

Slanting posts with notched ends can be bolted on edge to outside.

Slanting 2x4 posts can also be bolted in pairs to the ends of joists.

Railings serve an important safety function, preventing people from accidently falling off the deck. Local building codes typically stipulate specific requirements.They usually must be 36 inches high and should have openings no larger than 9 or 10 inches square to prevent small children from falling through. There are numerous creative solutions to satisfying the safety need for fill-in, several alternatives are illustrated below. The railings shown can be adapted to construct a wide variety of creative designs for railing fill-ins.

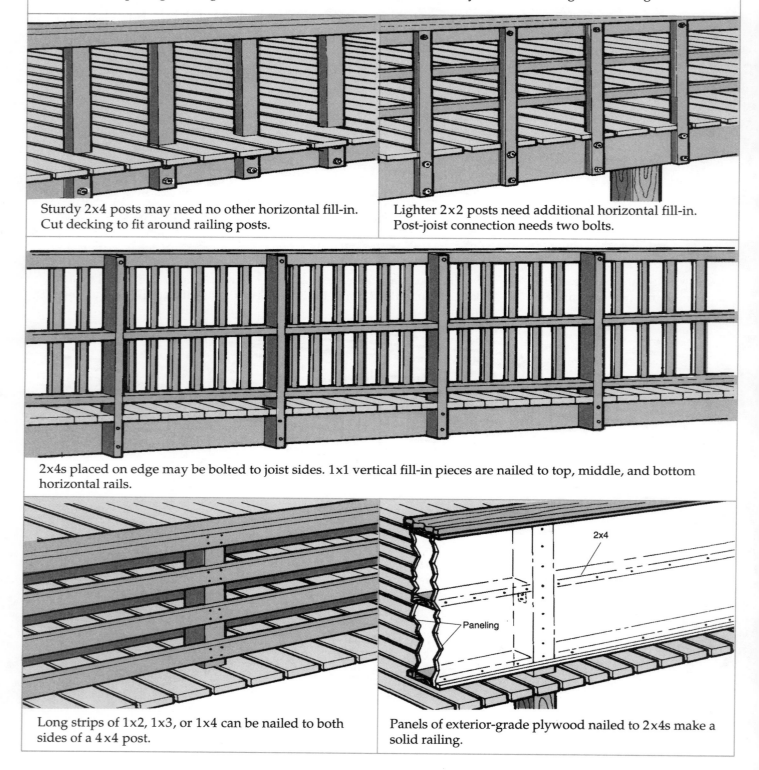

Sturdy 2x4 posts may need no other horizontal fill-in. Cut decking to fit around railing posts.

Lighter 2x2 posts need additional horizontal fill-in. Post-joist connection needs two bolts.

2x4s placed on edge may be bolted to joist sides. 1x1 vertical fill-in pieces are nailed to top, middle, and bottom horizontal rails.

Long strips of 1x2, 1x3, or 1x4 can be nailed to both sides of a 4x4 post.

Panels of exterior-grade plywood nailed to 2x4s make a solid railing.

BUILD: DECK BENCHES

Benches that are strategically placed around the deck are invitations for people to sit and relax. Not only can built-in benches double as railings, they also can divide the deck into separate areas for different activities. Whether they are bolted to the deck with braces, or hung off the railing supports with support bars, built-in benches add an attractive touch.

Building a Railing Bench

1

Installing the Support. A simple bench can be added to a railing by installing two-piece seat supports and bolting them to the railing posts and the joists. Cut the decking to fit around the vertical member.

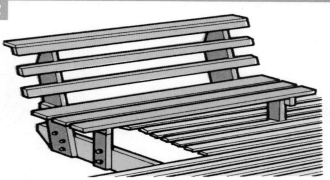

2

Attaching the Seat. Screw 2x6 boards to the seat supports. Make any splices in the seat with butt joints over the support, and add cleats underneath for more support.

Installing a Heavy Bench

1

Building the Support. In a more solid bench design the back rest, a 2x12 set in at a comfortable angle, is supported by 2x6s bolted to each joist. The seat support is attached at the decking with metal angles.

2

Making the Seat. Screw 2x2s to the horizontal 2x4s that provide the seat support. Leave a 1/4- or 1/2-in. space between the 2x2s. To splice the seating, make butt joints over the support and add cleats underneath for reinforcement.

Building a Low Bench

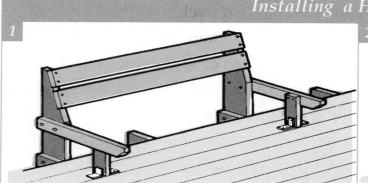

1

2 x 6s

Beam

Joist

Installing the Support. To build a comfortable bench where there is no railing, bolt T-shaped supports made from 2x6s to the joists. Notch the decking to fit around them.

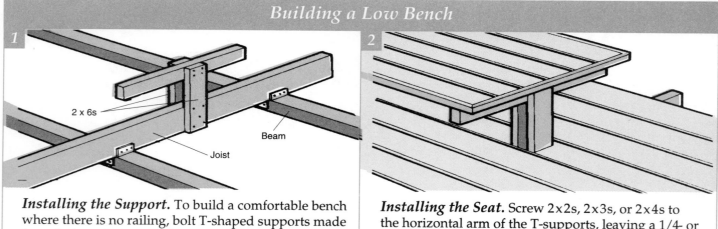

2

Installing the Seat. Screw 2x2s, 2x3s, or 2x4s to the horizontal arm of the T-supports, leaving a 1/4- or 1/2-in. space between the boards for drainage. For a decorative finish, screw 1x2s to the seat boards all

BUILD: STAIRS & RAMPS

Stairs provide access to a deck from the ground level or provide a connection between deck levels. If a deck is attached to a house, for convenience and safety, it is best to make the deck only an inch or two lower than the interior level. Establishing the right relation between the height of the step, called the rise, and the depth of the tread, called the run, is important for safety. Stairs that are too tall or too shallow cause accidents.

Stringer Support Stairs

1 **Designing Steps.** The parts of a set of stairs are identified at right. The steps, called treads, are supported by the stringers, which are fastened at the top to the joists or beams of the deck and at ground level to a concrete footing.

Establishing the right relation between the height of the step, called the rise, and the depth of the tread, called the run, is important for safety. Follow the instructions on page 69 to calculate rise and run.

2 **Making Footings.** To build a support for the bottom end of the stringers, excavate a 6- to 8-inch-deep trench that extends about 6 inches beyond the sides of the steps and 8 to 10 inches in front. Line the rim with a frame of 2x6 lumber. Tilt the frame slightly away from the deck to provide drainage for the footing. Fill the trench with concrete, level it, and put anchoring hardware in place.

3 **Attaching Stringers.** If the stringers run at right angles to the joists, attach them with metal connectors. If the joists and stringers are parallel, bolt them together. Use only galvanized fasteners. Bolt the bottoms of the stringers to the metal connectors in the concrete, or to the 4x4 post.

4 **Installing Risers.** Cut the risers from 2x lumber to fit the rise notches in the stringers exactly. The bottom of the riser rests on the stringer. Nail the risers in place with 12d galvanized nails. Note: The riser boards may be omitted if desired, to make a more open design.

5 **Installing Treads.** Cut the treads from 2x lumber; a 1-inch overhang in front is standard. Use several 2x4s or 2x6s, rather than larger boards, which are more likely to warp. Nail the treads in place with galvanized 16d nails. Place the best side of the treads up.

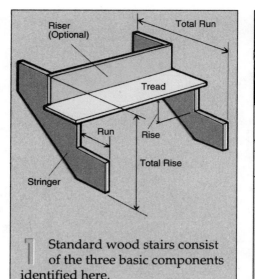

1 Standard wood stairs consist of the three basic components identified here.

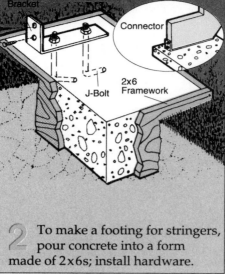

2 To make a footing for stringers, pour concrete into a form made of 2x6s; install hardware.

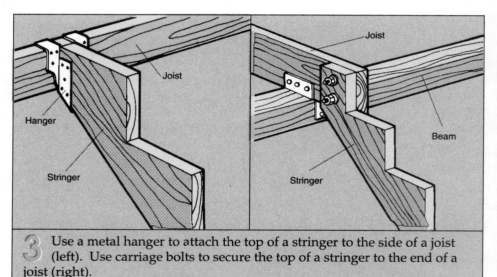

3 Use a metal hanger to attach the top of a stringer to the side of a joist (left). Use carriage bolts to secure the top of a stringer to the end of a joist (right).

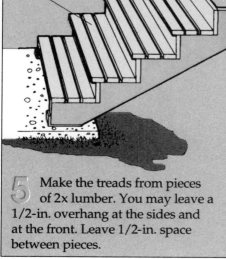

4 Cut the risers to fit the stringers; the top of the riser must be flush with the horizontal stringer cut.

5 Make the treads from pieces of 2x lumber. You may leave a 1/2-in. overhang at the sides and at the front. Leave 1/2-in. space between pieces.

Calculating the Rise and Run

Follow this rule of thumb: The depth of the tread plus twice the step height or rise should equal about 25 inches. A good combination for outdoor steps is a 6-inch rise with a 12- or 13-inch tread. Another is a 6½-inch rise with an 11- or 12-inch tread. The deeper the tread, the lower the rise. In any case, all steps must have identical measurements. Steps of varied sizes cause stumbles. A safe stairway must have a whole number of equal-size steps.

Determining Dimensions. Measure the total rise from ground level to deck level, the top surface of the decking; as an example, imagine it is 50 inches. Divide that by a convenient rise dimension, such as 6 inches: 50÷6=8+steps, which rounds off to 8. To get the exact rise of each step, divide the total rise again, this time by the rounded-off step number: 50÷8=6¼ inches.

To determine how far from the deck edge the stairs will extend on the ground, figure the total run: Subtract 1 from the number of steps (the deck will be the tread of the top step), and multiply by an appropriate tread depth, such as 12 inches. So the total run is: (8-1)×12=84 inches.

If you had rounded off the 8+step figure to 9 steps, the individual rise would be 50÷9=5½ inches, and with a 14-inch tread the total run would be (9-1)×14=112 inches.

A 7-inch rise is about the safe maximum for outdoor steps; a 5-inch rise is the safe minimum.

Treads should be at least 11 inches deep. The width of the stairs depends on use. If most traffic will be one person at a time, 40 inches is adequate. If most traffic will be pairs or groups of people, provide at least a 5-foot width. The supporting stringers, cut from 2x10s or, preferably, 2x12s, should be placed no more than 30 inches apart. So, for example, stairs 5 feet wide need three stringers. For a total run of more than 6 feet, use the stronger double-stringer design shown on page 70. Treat all lumber surfaces, fresh cuts, and bolt holes with preservative. Check building codes for local requirements in dimensions and railings as well as design.

Railings for Stairs & Ramps

All stairs and ramps up to 6 feet wide should have railings. Stairs of one or two steps, or very wide stairs and ramps, may not need railings. Check local codes.

1. Cut 4x4 posts and bolt them vertically to the stringers at the top and bottom, no more than 5 feet apart.

2. Run a chalk line across the posts parallel to the stringers and mark cut lines so that the top of the cap board will be at least 30 inches above the tread. Cut off the post tops with a circular saw.

3. Nail 2x4 or 2x6 cap boards to the post tops (see page 62). For fill-in install additional boards parallel to the stringers or perpendicular to the treads as desired.

4. Install additional horizontal or vertical fill-in boards as desired.

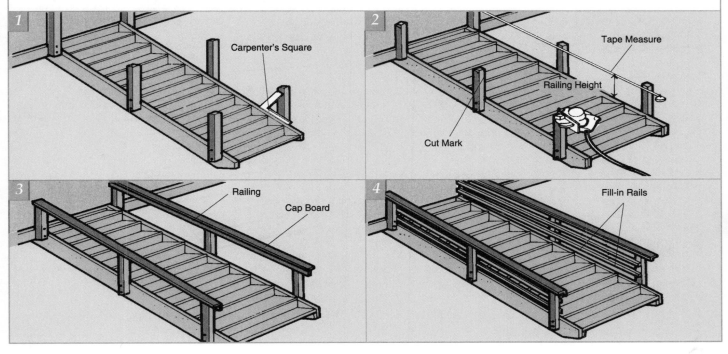

1 — Carpenter's Square

2 — Tape Measure / Railing Height / Cut Mark

3 — Railing / Cap Board

4 — Fill-in Rails

Double-Stringer Stairs

If the total run of your stairs is more than 6 feet, use double-stringer construction for additional support.

1 Cutting the Outer Stringers. For each double stringer, cut one solid outer stringer. Nail the stringers together with 10d nails.

2 Cutting the Inner Stringers. For each outer stringer cut one notched inner stringer.

3 Attaching Stringers. Nail or screw the stringer pairs together. Attach the top of the stringers to the joists (see page 68) and the bottoms to the footing. Build a concrete footing to support the stair bottom (see page 68).

4 Installing Risers and Treads. Cut risers and treads from 2x lumber to fit the notched stringer, and install as explained in Steps 4, page 68.

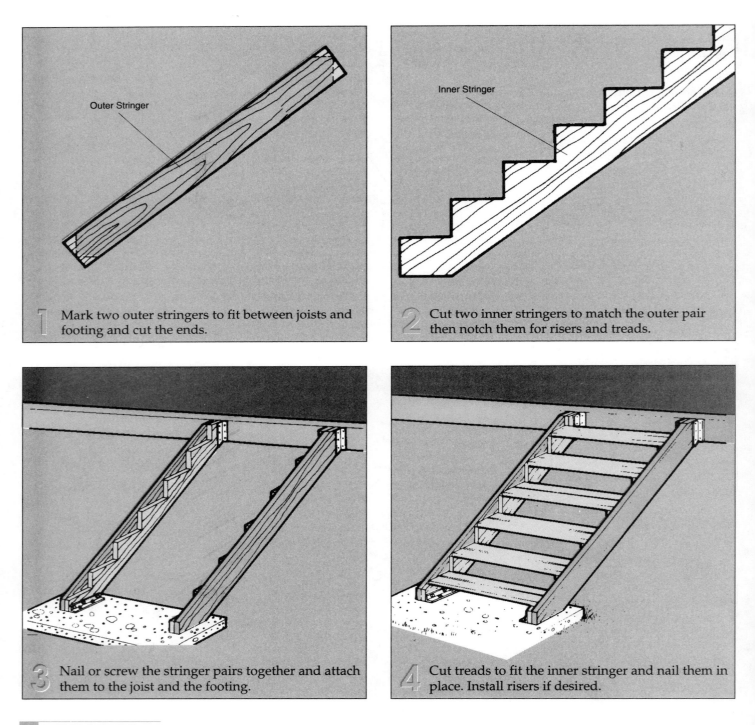

Outer Stringer

Inner Stringer

1 Mark two outer stringers to fit between joists and footing and cut the ends.

2 Cut two inner stringers to match the outer pair then notch them for risers and treads.

3 Nail or screw the stringer pairs together and attach them to the joist and the footing.

4 Cut treads to fit the inner stringer and nail them in place. Install risers if desired.

Cleat Support Stairs

This alternate basic stair design involves attaching wood cleats to the stringers to support the treads, rather than cutting notches for them.

1 Making the Stringers. Use a carpenter's square to mark the rise and run of each step on a 2x12. Cut only the top and bottom ends of the stringers.

2 Cutting and Attaching Cleats. Using 2x4 lumber, cut cleats to support the full depth of each tread on each stringer. Bolt the cleats to the inside of the stringers, aligned with

the mark made in Step 1, but with a 1/8-inch forward tilt for drainage.

3 Attaching the Stringers. If the stringers run at right angles to the joists, attach them with metal connectors. If the joists and stringers are parallel, bolt them together. Use only galvanized fasteners. Bolt the bottoms of the stringers to the metal connectors in the concrete footing (see page 68).

4 Installing the Treads. Cut treads from 2x4 or 2x6 lumber to fit snugly between the stringers. Screw the treads to the top of the cleats. Leave 1/2 inch between tread boards.

(see page 68)

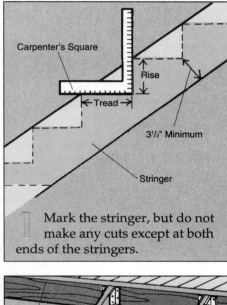

Mark the stringer, but do not make any cuts except at both ends of the stringers.

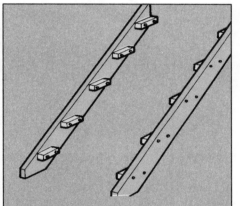

Bolt the cleats to the insides of stringers so the top of the cleat lies on the mark made in Step 1.

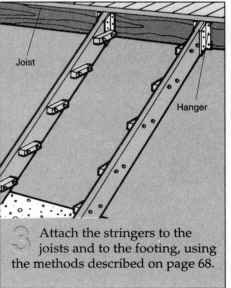

Attach the stringers to the joists and to the footing, using the methods described on page 68.

the methods described on page 68.

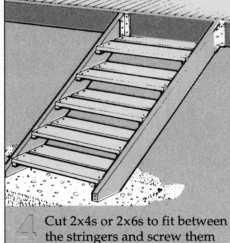

Cut 2x4s or 2x6s to fit between the stringers and screw them to the tops of the cleats. Leave 1/2 -in. space between tread boards.

Build Simple Box Steps

To join two deck levels separated by rise of less than 20 inches, or to provided access to a low-level deck, use simple box-like steps. If the total rise is no more than 14 inches, make one box step equal to half the rise. For a rise of no more than 19½ inches, make a two-step box. Toenail the steps to the deck levels, or provide a concrete slab for support.

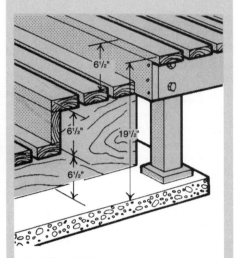

To fill a 19½-in. rise, make a two-step box. Cut stringers from 2x lumber, as shown above.

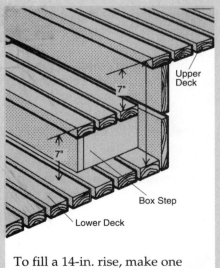

To fill a 14-in. rise, make one 7-in. box step: a three-sided form of 2x6s with 2x4 treads.

Build a Ramp

A ramp may be an attractive design alternative to stairs or a necessity for a person in a wheelchair. Local codes may be very specific in the latter case. Usually the run of a ramp must be eight times the rise. For example, if the total rise is 3 feet, the total run must be at least 24 feet.

1 Designing the Ramp. A ramp may be placed at right angles to a deck if you have the space; if not, it can be built parallel to the deck, as shown at right, with a wide top landing. The ramp should be 4 feet wide, and usually requires railings (see page 69).

2 Cutting the Stringers. Cut stringers from 2x12s. If you need to splice pieces, make butt joints reinforced with metal plates. Joints must rest on 4x4 posts on footings.

3 Making the Ramp Footing. Precast ramp footings are sometimes available. Or, build a wood form for concrete and insert connector hardware (see page 68).

4 Attaching Stringer to Footing. Bolt the bottom end of the stringers to the connector hardware embedded in the footing.

5 Attaching to Joist. Use joist hangers to join the stringers to the joist at right angles.

6 Installing the Decking. Nail 2x4 decking boards to the stringers with galvanized 10d nails. Leave 1/8-inch space between the boards, and 1/4-inch between the first board and footing.

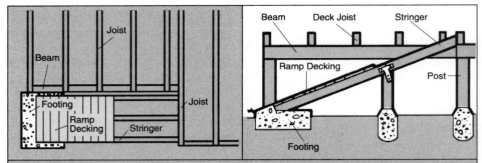

1 The plan drawing shows the relationship of ramps to the landing at the deck level (left). The elevation drawing (right) shows the stringers supported by footing, posts and joist.

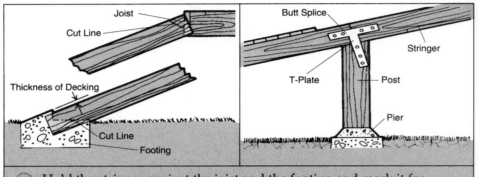

2 Hold the stringer against the joist and the footing and mark it for cutting (left). Splice stringers with a butt joint placed over a post and joined with metal T- plates (right).

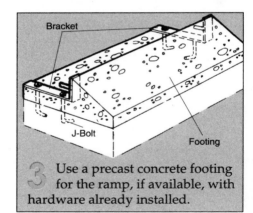

3 Use a precast concrete footing for the ramp, if available, with hardware already installed.

4 Join stringers to the footing connectors. Leave room for decking top to meet footing flush.

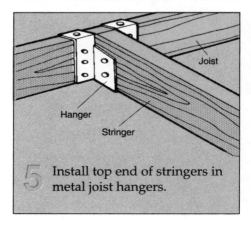

5 Install top end of stringers in metal joist hangers.

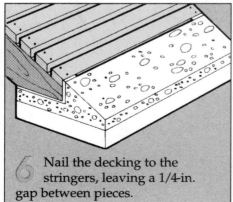

6 Nail the decking to the stringers, leaving a 1/4-in. gap between pieces.

BUILD: OVERHEAD COVER

A deck with an overhead cover is even more like an outdoor room. The roof structure defines the space but still allows a feeling of openness. Although the design and structural ideas shown are basic, they can be elaborated to create coverings to fill your own needs.

Building an Overhead Wood Structure

The deck covering shown here is integrated with a basic deck structure. The sizes of dimension lumber to be used for various structures are given in the chart opposite. The support posts may be secured as shown here or to the deck joists. These posts may be integrated with the deck railing (see pages 62-64).

1 **Setting up the Posts.** The posts for the overhead structure may be the same ones that support the deck. You may extend all the exterior deck posts or only widely spaced ones, as long as they meet support requirements. If the deck sits on the ground, without posts, or if you are adding a roof at a later time, attach the support posts to the deck with metal bases.

2 **Attaching the Beams.** In this design, pairs of 2x10s bolted to the posts form the main supporting beams. About 24 inches of overhang has been used at both ends. With a helper, first tack-nail the beams in place and then make sure they are properly aligned before fastening them permanently. The bottom of the beam should be at least 84 inches above the level of the deck.

3 **Setting the Purlins and Fascia.** The next level of the structure, called the purlins, consists of 2x6s set on edge at right angles to the beams and toenailed in place. In this design the purlins are 24 inches on center. If desired, 2x6 fascia boards can be nailed across the ends of the purlins, to provide additional stability.

4 **Installing Fill-In.** Latticework fill-in can be made from 2x2 strips of wood placed at right angles to or diagonally across the purlins. A second layer of 2x2s can be nailed to the first layer from underneath. A denser fill-in can be made from 1x4s nailed close together across the purlins; this creates a louvered cover.

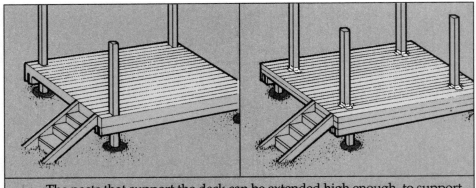

1 The posts that support the deck can be extended high enough to support the overhead (left) or posts can be set anywhere on the deck, using metal foot plates.

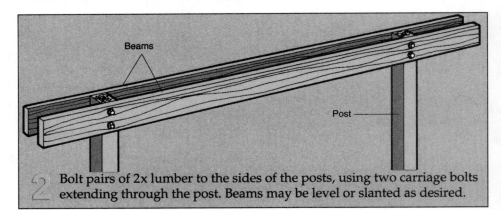

2 Bolt pairs of 2x lumber to the sides of the posts, using two carriage bolts extending through the post. Beams may be level or slanted as desired.

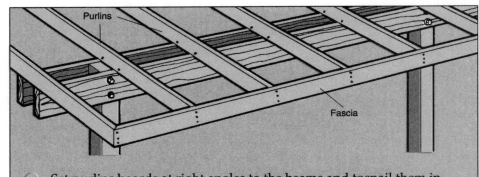

3 Set purlins boards at right angles to the beams and toenail them in place. Nail fascia boards across the ends of the purlins for stability.

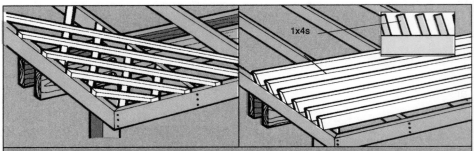

4 Pieces of 2x2 lumber can be nailed diagonally across purlins, or in a criss-cross pattern (left). To make a louvered cover, nail 1x4s with beveled edges at right angles to the purlins (right).

Additional Types of Fill-In

The basic overhead structure described on the previous page can support many different kinds of covering materials, including wood, plastic and canvas.

Lath Fill-In. Lathing is thin, narrow strips of flexible, lightweight wood. To make a deck covering, nail laths to the purlins with 1/2-inch spacing. This lets sun and rain filter through the cracks. This design can save tax dollars, since some communities do not categorize lath structures as permanent buildings and therefore impose no tax on them. If you use cedar or redwood lath, let the structure weather naturally. Otherwise, apply a coat of stain or paint.

Fiberglass Panels. Set the purlins 24 inches on center to accommodate the standard 26-inch fiberglass panels, which will overlap one corrugation on each side. Also, give the purlins a good pitch, that is, let the roof rise about 3 inches for every 12 inches of span. This provides adequate drainage of rain and snow. To prevent sagging, add cross bracing every 5 feet between the purlins. Use aluminum nails and neoprene washers to attach the panels to the purlins. Predrill the nail holes.

Canvas Covering. In dry climates a canvas overhead cover will last a long time and provide shade and rain protection at a relatively low cost. The easiest installation method is to tie the stretched fabric to a wood frame or to a pipe frame, as shown right. The canvas can be hemmed at an awning shop, or you can sew up to No. 10 weight canvas yourself, using a No. 13 sailmaker's needle and Dacron thread. The awning shop can also put in grommets, or you can do it yourself, using a grommet die and die block. A tied-on canvas cover requires grommets placed every 8 inches and at each corner.

Use 1/4-inch diameter cord or rope to lash the canvas to a framework.

Roof Structural Requirements

For roof to be supported by house on one or more sides, without overhang.

ROOF AREA	RAFTERS Spacing	RAFTERS Size	BEAMS Number	BEAMS Size	POSTS* Number	POSTS* Spacing
8'x16'	12" o.c.	8'2"x4"	2	8'2"x8"	3	8' o.c.
	16" o.c.	8'2"x4"	2	8'4"x6"	Same	
	24" o.c.	8'2"x6"	1	16'2"x14"	2	16'o.c.
8'x24'	Same		2	12'2"x10"	4	8' o.c.
			2	12'4"x6"	Same	
			3	8'2"x8"	5	6' o.c.
10'x16'	16" o.c.	10'2"x6"	2	8'2"x8"	3	8' o.c.
	24" o.c.	10'2"x6"	2	8'4"x6"	Same	
10'x24'	Same		2	12'2"x12"	3	12' o.c.
12'x16'	12" o.c.	12'2"x6"	2	8'2"x10"	3	8' o.c.
	16" o.c.	12'2"x6"	2	8'4"x6"	Same	
	24" o.c.	12'2"x8"	1	16'4"x12"	2	16' o.c.
12'x24'	Same		2	12'2"x12"	3	12' o.c.
			2	12'4"x8"	4	8" o.c.
16'x16'	16" o.c.	16'2"x8"	2	8'2"x10"	3	8' o.c.
	24" o.c.	16'2"x10"	1	16'4"x14"	2	16' o.c.
16'x24'	Same		3	8'2"x10"	4	8' o.c.
			3	8'4"x8"	Same	
			2	12'2"x14"	3	12' o.c.

*Use 4x4 posts for spacing up to 5 feet, 4x6 posts for spacing from 6 to 8 feet, and 6x6 posts for spacing over 8 feet.

Additional Types of Overhead Cover

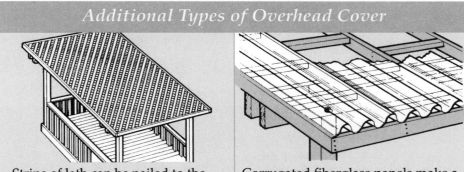

Strips of lath can be nailed to the purlins to make as dense or as open a cover as desired.

Corrugated fiberglass panels make a long-lasting lightweight cover. Pitch for adequate drainage.

Canvas Deck Covering

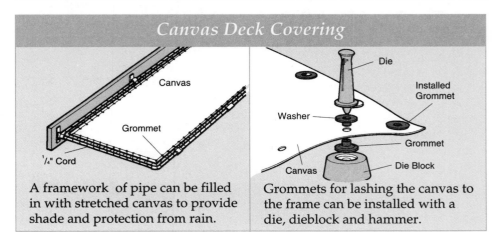

A framework of pipe can be filled in with stretched canvas to provide shade and protection from rain.

Grommets for lashing the canvas to the frame can be installed with a die, dieblock and hammer.

Building a Retractable Canvas Deck Cover

If your deck needs only occasional protection from sun and rain, consider this adjustable awning designed by the California Redwood Association. The heavyweight canvas awning extends and retracts by a rope and pulley system. It can be installed on the overhead framework described in this chapter, provided the purlins are pitched to give adequate runoff. Use canvas in the normal 76-inch width, or sew narrower panels together to fit.

1 Creating Dowel Tunnels. Sew folds across the canvas, using 3½ inches of material, to make dowel tunnels; leave 14 inches between seams. Double-stitch each seam. Cut lengths of 3/4-inch doweling to fit the width of your canvas strip, and insert them in the tunnels.

2 Installing Screw Eyes. Put three screw eyes through the canvas tunnel into each dowel opposite the seam. The screw eyes should match the spacing of the pipe supports. Use tent wall snaps to connect each screw eye to a metal ring on the pipe.

3 Installing Support Pipes. Use three 1/2-inch galvanized metal pipes to support each awning strip. The pipes run at right angles to the roof slope. Slip 1½-inch metal rings over the pipes, enough to support each dowel; put half the rings in each side of the center support. Use screw hooks at the ends and in the center of each pipe to secure it to the purlins.

4 Installing the Control Rope. Connect the control rope to the center ring at both ends of the awning, so that the halves move in opposite directions when the rope is pulled, opening and closing to and from the center.

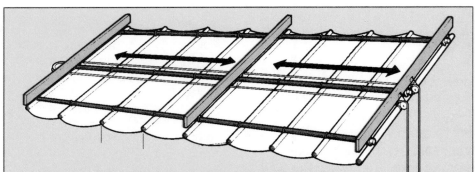

Designing a Retracting Canvas Deck Cover. Sheets of canvas, sewn to dowels that are hung from pipes, open and close in two sections, controlled by ropes running on pulleys.

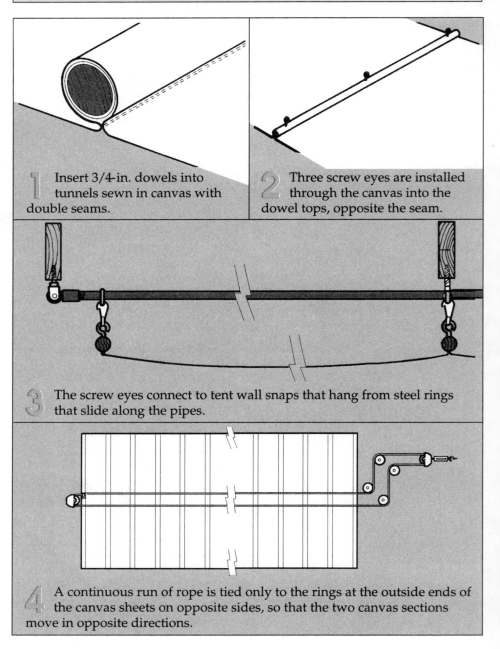

1 Insert 3/4-in. dowels into tunnels sewn in canvas with double seams.

2 Three screw eyes are installed through the canvas into the dowel tops, opposite the seam.

3 The screw eyes connect to tent wall snaps that hang from steel rings that slide along the pipes.

4 A continuous run of rope is tied only to the rings at the outside ends of the canvas sheets on opposite sides, so that the two canvas sections move in opposite directions.

WOOD DECK MAINTENANCE

Even a well-built deck can have problems. The accumulation of dirt, leaves and moisture leads to wood decay. Shade and moisture encourage mildew and fungus. Normal wear and tear may loosen joints and connections and damage wood surfaces. Wood color and texture deteriorate through the weathering effects of sun, rain, freezing and thawing, as well as through normal use. In addition to proper care, long life for a wood deck begins with the good design and construction techniques described previously.

Maintenance Procedures

To give your deck longer life, follow these maintenance procedures:

▨ Sweep the deck often; hose it down when dirt accumulates.

▨ Clean the cracks between deck boards in the fall when the leaves have fallen, and in the spring before the busy season. Use a stiff wire or a putty knife.

▨ Remove mildew promptly. It can appear as dirt-like spots, but grows into larger black or brown stains. Use a mildewcide annually or more often on shaded areas.

▨ Check annually for wood rot and replace any damaged pieces. Coat any new pieces and cuts with wood preservative.

▨ To restore the natural color of wood, brush on a dilute solution of oxalic acid. Add 4 ounces of acid to a gallon of water; use rubber gloves. When this solution has dried, hose off the deck thoroughly.

▨ To accelerate the weathering process, or to match new wood to weathered wood, apply a solution of one part baking soda in five parts water. Wash the deck down the following day.

▨ Apply a coat of wood stain or water repellent a minimum of every two years. In areas of severe weather conditions, more frequent applications may be necessary.

Cleaning the Deck

Scrub down the desk surface at least twice a year, especially after the leaves fall, to remove dirt and decaying matter

Dig dirt and rotting leaves out of the cracks between decking boards before the boards themselves begin to decay.

Repairing the Decking

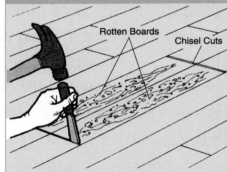
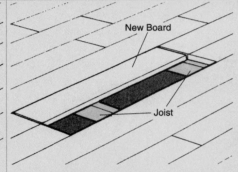

Chisel out all sections of rotting boards with a wood chisel and hammer. Cut new pieces to fit and coat them with wood preservative.

Nail new boards securely in place. The ends of all pieces should be nailed to joists or to blocking added between joists.

Preserving the Decking

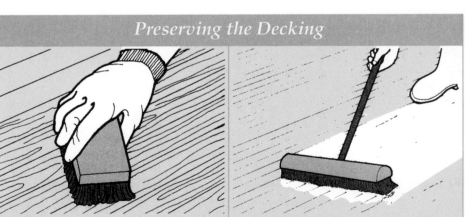
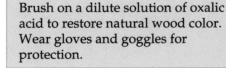

Brush on a dilute solution of oxalic acid to restore natural wood color. Wear gloves and goggles for protection.

In areas of severe weather, and for decks that get heavy use, apply a coat of wood stain or water repellent a minimum of every two years.

Backfill (Noun) Earth, sand or gravel used to fill the excavated space under a deck, patio, or other structure. (Verb) The process of doing the above.

Batter board A structure consisting of stakes and crosspieces to which you attach strings for achieving square corners when building decks.

Beam A large framing member attached horizontally to the posts, used to support joists.

Blocking Short pieces of joist lumber inserted at right angles between joists to strengthen them.

Board foot Unit of lumber measurement: a quantity of wood 12" x 12" x 1" (see Linear foot).

Bridging Pieces of lumber fastened in an X pattern between joists to prevent twisting.

Butt Joint Two pieces of wood joined by attaching the square-cut end of one member to the end or face of another.

Cantilever Construction that extends out beyond its vertical support.

Chalk line String or cord covered with chalk that is snapped against wood members to make a mark for measurement or cutting.

Clinch To drive overlong nails through boards and bend the points down flat on the other side.

Cleat A short length of wood fastened to a joist, post, or other framing member to support a ledger or railing, for example.

Curing The slow chemical action that hardens concrete.

Decking Boards or plywood nailed to joists to form the deck surface.

Dimension lumber Pieces of wood cut and milled to standard sizes (see Nominal dimensions).

Dry well Gravel-filled hole used to receive and drain water runoff.

Duplex nail A double-head nail used for temporary wood framing or bracing; easily pulled out by the top head.

Elevation Drawing or view of construction showing its vertical members or faces.

Expansion shield Metal connector driven into masonry to hold a fastener, such as a bolt.

Fascia Board facing that covers the exposed ends and sides of decking to provide a finished appearance.

Flashing Preformed strips of aluminum or galvanized metal attached to the topside of a ledger or other component to repel water.

Footing The part of a foundation or support system that is in direct contact with the earth.

Frost line The level below grade (q.v.) beneath which the ground does not freeze.

Galvanizing Coating a metal with a thin layer of zinc to prevent rust. Connectors and fasteners must be galvanized for outdoor use.

Grade The ground level. On-grade means at or on the natural ground level.

Header In deck construction, a board attached across the ends of the joists to prevent them from twisting; in walls, a heavy horizontal member placed across the top of door and window openings to support the roof structure above.

Joist Structural member placed perpendicular across beams to support deck boards.

Joist hanger Metal connector used to join a joist and a beam or ledger so that the tops of both are on the same level.

Lag screw/lag bolt A large hex-head screw used to fasten framing members face-to-face; typically used for joining horizontal framing members to posts or exterior walls.

Lath Thin, narrow strips of wood used for filling in screens, trellises and roofs.

Ledger Board attached horizontally to the wall of an existing structure, to which you attach deck joists.

Linear foot Unit of lumber measurement consisting of a piece of wood 1 foot. long, of any dimension size (see Board foot).

Miter Joint A joint in which the ends of two boards are cut at equal angles (typically 45 degrees) to form a corner

Nominal dimensions The identifying dimensions of a piece of lumber (e.g., 2x4) which are larger than the actual dimensions (11/2" X 31/2").

On center A point of reference for measuring. "16 inches on center" means 16 inches from the center of one joist, for example, to the center of the next joist.

Penny (abbr. d) Unit of nail measurement; e.g., a 10d nail is 3 inches long.

Plan view Drawing or view of a structure from an overhead perspective (i.e., top view).

Plumb Vertically straight, in relation to a horizontally level surface.

Post Vertical framing member (e.g a 4 x 4 or 6 x 6) set on the foundation to support the beams of a deck.

Purlin A horizontal structural roof member which supports rafters.

Riser Vertical boards placed between stringers on stairs to support stair treads.

Run On stairs, the horizontal distance between one riser (q.v.) and the next.

Running foot (see Linear foot).

Shim Small, wedged piece of wood driven between two framing members (e.g. beams and joists) to level or otherwise position them.

Skirt Solid band of horizontal wood members (fascia) installed around the deck perimeter to conceal exposed ends of joists and deck boards.

Skirt joist A joist installed across the ends of other joists for additional stability.

Saddle anchor Metal connector that secures a joist to the top of a beam.

Stringer On stairs, the diagonal boards that support the treads and risers; also called a stair horse.

Stud anchor A headless threaded fastener with an expandable tip, inserted into a hole drilled in wood or masonry; the projecting threaded end enables you to attach a ledger by means of a nut and washer.

Tacknail To nail one structural member to another temporarily with a minimum of nails.

Toenail To nail two pieces of wood together by driving nails at an angle through the edge of one into the other.

Tread On stairs, the horizontal boards supported by the stringers.